AWAKE TO RACISM

JOANN MALONE

Copyright © 2021 by Joann Malone

All rights reserved.

No part of this book may be reproduced in any form or by any electronic or mechanical means, including information storage and retrieval systems, without written permission from the author, except for the use of brief quotations in a book review.

Paperback ISBN 978-1-7365588-0-5

Cover Photo by Kathy Karn

Author Photo by Patrick Smith

Cover Design by Freddy Bosche

Publishing Assistance Provided by:

Michelle Morrow www.chellreads.com

Some names have been changed to protect the privacy of the person named.

"Whether as a soul storyteller or as an insightful analyst of the nation's racial realities, Joann Malone has written a book certain to educate all of us and endure as a literary treasure."

— COLMAN MCCARTHY, *I'D RATHER TEACH PEACE*.

"Joann Malone has written a powerful, inspiring and passionate book, a must read."

— RUTH FISHEL M.ED., *TIME FOR JOY, TIME FOR PEACE* AND MANY OTHER BOOKS.

"An extraordinary adventure by an unlikely superhero - with deep and thoughtful insight that deserves a place on the nation's bookshelves."

— TIM BROWN, FORMER ATTORNEY TURNED WRITER, AUTHOR AND PHILOSOPHER.

"Joann provides a dynamic and lyrical quilt of activism that has been woven throughout her life while seeking community, peace, and personal growth."

— NICOLE BURTON, *SWIMMING UP THE SUN*

CONTENTS

Introduction	xi
How Can I Help?	1
"I Can't Breathe!"	3
Awakening in Alabama	11
My Beautiful People	23
Becoming an Ally to Black Power	33
Action Against War and Racism	45
A Minority in Jail	53
My White Privilege 2020	63
Speaking Out against War, Racism, Corporate Killing	67
Murdered in Their Beds	77
In Cook County Men's Jail	85
The Prison Project	95
D.C. Fight Back	107
Living in a Black Family	119
Recovery	129
Just Mercy	139
Teaching/The Diversity Workshop	153
Listening to My Diversity Workshop Students	169
More Teachers on Antiracism	191
African-American Heroes Inspire Us	197
LET THE GRANDCHILDREN SPEAK!!!	205
How to Build Beloved Communities	215
What do we do to end Racism?	231
Say Their Names	247
Resources	257
My profound gratitude:	269
About the Author	273

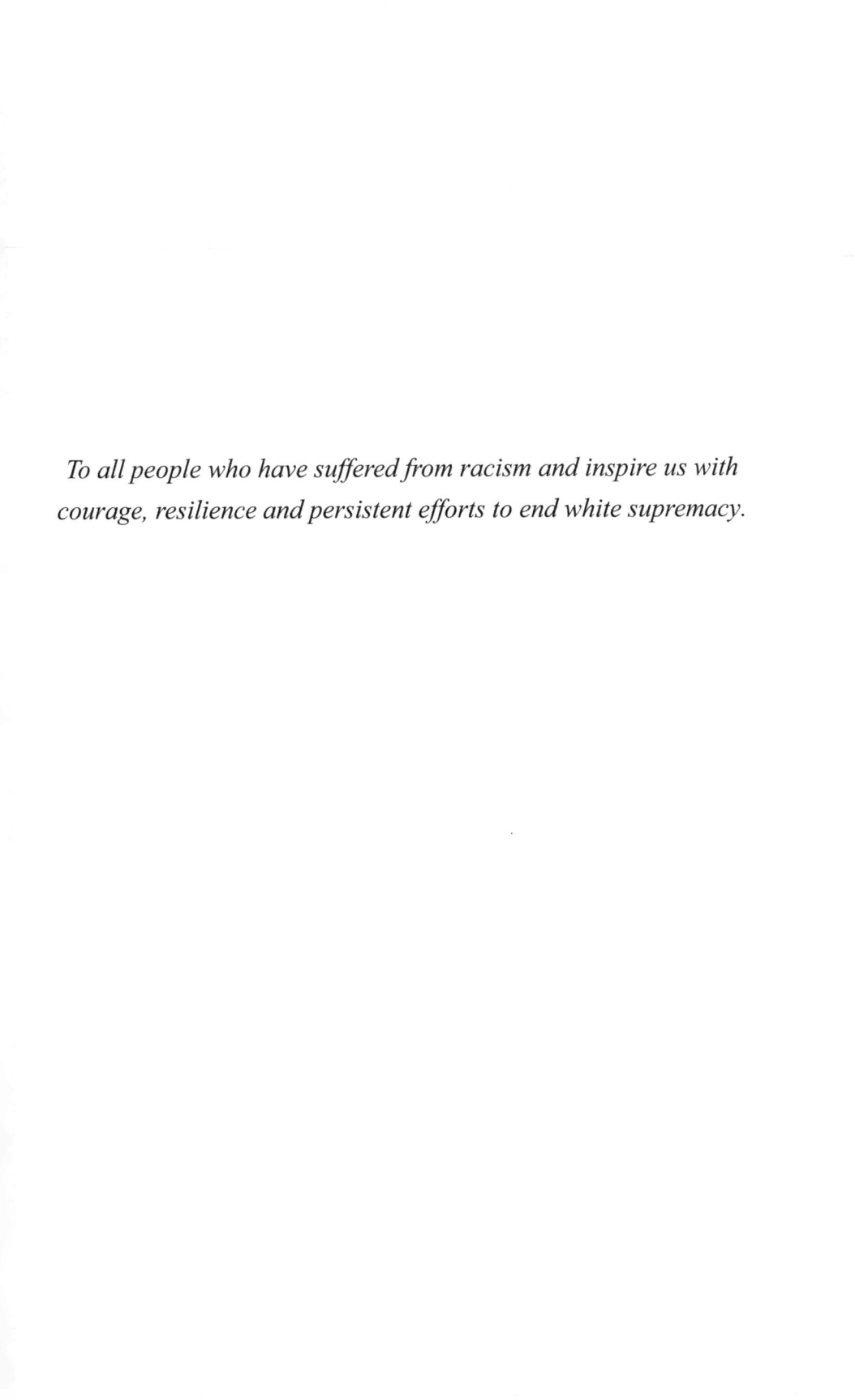

To all people who have suffered from racism and inspire us with courage, resilience and persistent efforts to end white supremacy.

We are all flawed and all human. We all have made mistakes and harmed others. We will again. We find it easier to practice forgiveness when we can recognize that the roles could have been reversed. Each of us could have been the perpetrator rather than the victim. Each of us has the capacity to commit the wrongs against others that were committed against us. Although I might say, "I would never . . ." genuine humility will answer, "Never say never." Rather say, "I hope that, given the same set of circumstances, I would not . . ." But can we ever really know?"

— *Desmond Tutu and Mpho Tutu*

INTRODUCTION

I am relying on the voices of all the People of Color in my life to speak in me, through me, in this white body to others who can help us stop the racist oppression of people because of their skin color, their national origin, their language, education, class, gender, whatever seems to divide us.

Most of those divisions are man-made and are constantly changing. Waking up to both the horrors of white supremacy and to the beauty of a multicultural beloved community has been a long process in my life. I would like to extend my hand to anyone on their own journey of waking up, listening, learning, experiencing, making mistakes, loving, and standing up with African Americans on the road to unity and justice.

HOW CAN I HELP?

On May 25, 2020, the world awoke to George Floyd's dying cries, "I can't breathe." African American communities felt the policeman's knee on their neck. The rest of the world experienced the brutality, the injustice, and cruelty over and over again in one continuous video loop. Around the world, the streets screamed in unison, "We can't breathe," but this reaction was just the beginning.

Seeing the slow murder roused people to demonstrate in the streets, to scream back "We can't breathe!" Millions were already experiencing the loneliness, fear, and panic of the Covid-19 pandemic sweeping the nation and the world. But many people, Black and white, young and old, took the chance of exposure to gather and speak out strongly against this latest racist murder. The White House reacted with more violence, unmarked troops beating, gassing and arresting people in Washington, D.C. and Portland, Oregon. The dividing lines in our country intensified.

A week later, I found myself in a writing workshop with the goal of producing a book in six months. I could have revised books I had already written, but the issue of racism was burning in my heart. My eightieth birthday looming, vulnerable to the pandemic, I had been completely sequestered since mid-March. It was difficult not to join the protests, to help paint "Black Lives Matter" on the street near the White House. I wanted to be there, to hear the voices, to connect with friends, to stand up and act as an antiracist. What I could do was write.

I contacted my granddaughter, finishing her sophomore year of university, sequestered by Covid in her parents' basement. I asked her "How can I help?" She responded with suggestions of places to donate funds, books to read, films to see, guidelines for white allies of People of Color like herself. The summer and fall became both a writing/daily publishing workshop, and a deeper course of study of how to be an antiracist in the 21st century.

I had grown up in complete segregation and ignorance, unaware of racism. There must be others like me who were just now waking up to its ugly reality. Would sharing my journey to awareness and hearing the voices of those who inspired me, help others?

"I CAN'T BREATHE!"
MAY 25, 2020

"I Can't BREATHE!"

Mama, Mama…I can't..
My neck hurts…everything hurts..
Please, I can't breathe, officer…
They're gonna kill me…
I can't breathe...
Please, sir, please…
I can't breathe."

Posted by u/holladollameatballa Black Lives Matter, me, watercolor, colored pencils, gouache on paper, 2020

Six minutes of pleading, crying out, then silence for the last three minutes as Derek Chauvin kept kneeling on the neck of a shackled George Floyd.

Millions heard the dying cries, as yet another Black man was killed by a white police officer. Thousands marched into the streets of the world's major cities. Floyd's voice was honored on city streets, in churches, and in meditations online where we breathed in silence for the time it took for him to die. Tears of grief and disbelief. The reaction was palpable - anger, fear for our children, determination to make this suffering stop.

Black people reacted and marched, but so did others. Hearing his words, seeing the video viewed repeatedly throughout the world touched the minds and hearts of white people also.

This killing was an unbelievable shock to some, a first awakening to the reality and depth of racism in our country. For African Americans, George Floyd's death represented the latest installment of thousands of similar deaths caused by police, prison guards or lynch mobs (*Washington Post*, 2020). They have been telling stories and repeating the names of sons, daughters, husbands unjustly targeted, arrested, beaten, and killed over the last four centuries.

Many of us had learned the history of slavery, the deaths during the Middle Passage, the cruelty, beatings, selling of children from their mothers' arms. Have we forgotten the Civil War fought to maintain the slavery of Black people? The brutality involved in destroying Reconstruction?

This summer I have been reading and listening to Black voices, reminding me of this history.

In *Stamped from the Beginning: The Definitive History of Racist Ideas* in America, Ibram X. Kendi describes another year of presidential election, that of Ulysses S. Grant in 1872. The recognition of the end of slavery and Reconstruction's attempts to enable Black political power ended with an armed defense of Republican-elected politicians. In Colfax, Louisiana, sixty-one armed Blacks barricaded themselves inside a courthouse on Easter Sunday, 1873. Democrats (the defenders of slavery at that time) shelled the courthouse with gunfire and executed the thirty-seven survivors.

From 1889-1929 a Black person was lynched on an average of every four days. These executions were ritualistic slaughters witnessed by white men, women and children watching the torture, killing and dismemberment of innocent Black people.

- Are most white people in the US raised on racial myths of inferiority of people of color?
- Were we trained to hate, discriminate against, blame, become immune to the cries of Black voices?
- What has that training, the lies and myths of our racial superiority done to us that we are capable of becoming murderers?

We resist being responsible for these murders. We say, "Not me! I'm not a murderer." But have we become immune to the reality of murder committed in our name? With our tax dollars? In our prisons? On our city streets? Justified in the name of our security, safety, and "normalcy"? We have a choice to listen, to watch with eyes open, to learn the truth and to stand up now against injustice.

May George Floyd's cry "I can't breathe" penetrate our hearts, open our minds to study our true history and give us courage to stop the killing and the policies protecting the killers.

My education about racism has been a process of seeing, hearing, connecting with real people, and learning from them what to do. Making mistakes. Learning more from the mistakes. Listening more, and opening my heart to change.

57th Anniversary March on Washington

August 29, 2020

Last August thousands gathered again at the Lincoln Memorial for the March on Washington for Racial Justice and Police Reform: "Get Your Knees Off Our Necks." Fifty-seven years after the 1963 March for Jobs and Freedom, where Dr. Martin Luther King, Jr delivered his famous "I Have a Dream" speech, we still need to fight for an end to police brutality and murders, the right for everyone to vote, equality in jobs, healthcare, education and the courts.

Pleas for peaceful protest came from the brother of George Floyd, the son of Eric Garner, the father of Ahmaud Arbery, and the mother of Trayvon Martin who said,

"Even though it looks dark, I want to tell you to be encouraged. Stand up. We were built for this!"

Dr. Martin Luther King, Jr's son spoke a similar message:

"We need you to vote as if your lives, our livelihoods, our liberties depend on it. Because they do," he told the crowd.

"There's a knee upon the neck of democracy, and our nation can only live so long without the oxygen of freedom."

It should not surprise us that we still need to cry out for an end to brutal killings of Black people, unjust imprisonments, voter intimidation and deprivation of basic human rights. This oppression is rooted in the four hundred year old history of slavery, brutality and injustice against African Americans. Each generation must take up the fight until we reach the promised land, a "beloved community" of which Dr. King speaks so eloquently.

I am still so deeply moved by his dream -

> "… one day right there in Alabama little black boys and black girls will be able to join hands with little white boys and white girls as sisters and brothers."

> "… one day on the red hills of Georgia, the sons of former slaves and the sons of former slave owners will be able to sit down together at the table of brotherhood."

If we are weary, cynical about the possibility of change, afraid, angry, hesitant that we have something to offer, we listen to these courageous, inspiring words and know there is a path. There are leaders, ancestors who have shown us the way. We need to keep putting one foot in front of the other - together. We are reminded that violent responses to violence don't work.

"We must forever conduct our struggle on the high plane of dignity and discipline. We must not allow our creative protest to degenerate into physical violence. Again and again, we must rise to the majestic heights of meeting physical force with soul force."

"And when this happens, and when we allow freedom to ring, when we let it ring from every village and every hamlet, from every state and every city, we will be able to speed up that day when all of God's children, black men and white men, Jews and Gentiles, Protestants and Catholics, will be able to join hands and sing in the words of the old Negro spiritual:

Free at last! Free at last!

Thank God Almighty, we are free at last!"

— 'I HAVE A DREAM' SPEECH, IN ITS ENTIRETY

The words from Martin Luther King's "I Have a Dream" speech rang in my ears as I made my first journey into the Deep South and into an awareness that would change my life…"I have a dream that my four little children will one day live in a nation where they will not be judged by the color of their skin but by the content of their character."

AWAKENING IN ALABAMA

Excited, nervous, trying to appear calm and "proper" in my long, black serge dress and veil, I sat stiffly on the train seat next to Sr. Ann Frederick. My body rattled and jerked to one side then the other as the train sped away from my home of three years at the Motherhouse in Kentucky.

Everything was new, strange, forbidding. I couldn't look the mother across the aisle from me in the eye, smile, sympathize with her struggling three-year old. We were supposed to keep "modesty of the eyes," not look directly at anyone, not speak unless spoken to. But the little boy kept giggling, whispering in his mother's ear, pointing at me, making me laugh. "Open the book on your lap, Joann, pretend to read," my conscience suggested.

Suddenly, we heard the screech of brakes, conductors screaming, "Sit now!" Boxes tumbling from the racks above our heads into our laps, the little boy thrust to the floor, rolling toward the open door. I leapt up, flopped on the ground, grabbed his ankle and pulled him into my arms as both of us were tossed back into the car by another jerk of the train.

Both of us were crying, holding one another, his mother now on the floor with us, reaching for her son. All pretense of "decorum" had flown out the door of the car.

The train had run into a cow! Or a cow ambled over the tracks and stood with big, brown cow eyes, watching the train speed toward it, a comet taking its life in an instant.

Changing mine forever.

Fortunately the train wreck happened close enough to the Birmingham, Alabama station that we could walk along the tracks, carrying our suitcases, bundles of food, water and umbrellas to shield us from the August sun. Sister Ann Frederick kept up a constant stream of anxious chatter, wondering what we would do, how we would be able to get to Montgomery. I kept stumbling on the stones by the tracks, my ugly black shoes now scuffed and covered with red dust.

When we arrived at the station, the two of us looked more like war refugees than nuns, our white collars and brims of our veils filthy with sweat. But the people there welcomed us, took our bags, showed us benches to hold our aching bodies, bathrooms to wash off the worst of the dust, gave us cold sodas to drink. Exhausted, we slumped on the pew-shaped bench and took our look at the Deep South.

I knew there were more African Americans in the South than in Missouri where I had grown up. But as I glanced at the porters, the clerks behind the glass windows of the ticket area, the children rolling a ball back and forth on the floor, tired mothers watching them, men stretched out on benches asleep, I realized we were the only white people there. Where had the others from the train, the mother and little boy sitting near us gone? A kind porter brought our bags to us and showed us a telephone booth where we could call the convent in Montgomery.

We waited two hours for our nuns to drive to Birmingham to fetch us. We read, we nodded, used the bathroom to wipe away more sweat and enjoyed the meager food available - hot dogs rotating on a spit, chips, pickles and more soda.

Curious, I asked a mother with two children to tell us where she lived, why she was traveling. She had lost her job in a factory in Birmingham, was going back to the farm further south where her parents still share-cropped. At least they could feed the children who might be able to help with the farm work.

"And you, where are you ladies going?" she asked.

"We're Sisters of Loretto," I replied.

"I'm going to teach at a small Catholic High School in Montgomery - Latin, Religion, and English. It's my first full-time teaching assignment."

"Ahh," she said, "Martin Luther King's city! Where the bus boycott happened in '55-'56, right after that boy was murdered in Mississippi."

"Emmett Till. Yes, he was a few months younger than me," I recalled... killed the summer before 10th grade."

"Oh! Oh, my LORD!" Sister Angelina squealed. "Oh, my dear LORD!" What are you doing on this side of the station? We've been looking for you for twenty minutes! What are you doing on the Negro side?" Squat, plump, freckled, Sr. Angelina was the picture of the proper nun, stiff, wide-eyed with horror at our indiscretion.

Sr Frederick and I let our heads drop to take the scolding but smiled at one another. We didn't know the rules of the South, clearly! Had no idea that we had spent the last two hours on the "Negro-only" side of a totally segregated train station. Apparently, the signs above the water fountains and bathrooms had been removed a year before, an after effect of the bus boycott. We just didn't know. It did explain what happened to all the other white passengers from our train. But not a soul in the room had made us feel different or unacceptable. They might have been smiling to themselves, but every act toward us was kindness itself.

Piling our bags into the trunk of the car, I looked back at the train station, knowing my life had shifted. What was I going to encounter here in the Deep South?

Sister Mary Madaleva Malone, changed her name to her given name, Sister Joann Malone after her first year of teaching (and teasing by her students).

On the ride to Montgomery, I couldn't get the story of Emmett Till out of my mind. How had I missed his story in high school?

It wasn't until much later that I saw the photos of his mangled body, beaten, shot, mutilated, bloated from being thrown into the Tallahatchie River in Mississippi, tied to a fan. Fourteen years old in 1954. Why hadn't I known more about him as a child?

"Emmett Till was my George Floyd."

John Lewis, before his death July 17, 2020

He should have been my George Floyd too. My age! But I was a white girl, ignorant of the issue of racism. I heard little about either Emmett Till or the Central High Nine in high school. I was focused on studies, dancing, boys, and the secrets in my family - my father's drinking, losing his job, beating my mother, my bailing him out of jail. I was unaware that our private girls' high school had been integrated in 1947 (seven years before Brown v. Board of Education) or that we had several African American students. They didn't affect my life. I didn't know them.

"My George Floyd was the four little girls killed in Birmingham"

Montgomery, Alabama, 1963

September 15, 1963: Addie Mae Collins, Cynthia Wesley, Carole Robertson and Carol Denise McNair, aged 11-14 years old.

The four girls, Addie Mae, Cynthia, Carole, and Carol Denise, were close to my youngest brother's age, blown apart by dynamite planted by Ku Klux Klan members, none of whom were prosecuted until 1977. The blast wounded over twenty others. Thousands of local African American people arrived at the 16th St. Baptist Church to dig out bodies, help the wounded. Many of the police were members of the same Ku Klux Klan that set this bomb and others.

I didn't know these little girls personally, but a few weeks before I had left Birmingham, and now lived two hours from the bombing, from attack dogs released on demonstrators by our Governor George Wallace. It was the top news on television, upsetting the white students I taught. They wanted to discuss what happened and had questions I couldn't answer. Some students remembered Martin Luther King and Rosa Parks' bus boycott years earlier. I asked them to tell me more, what had they experienced when they had no bus service for months? Were they as shocked as I was that anyone could deliberately kill young Black girls, much less dynamite a church?

I sought out my two new friends, the only people my age I knew in this new life. I had gravitated toward Amy, the cook in our small convent of fifteen women, all much older than me. She and the janitor in the school, Buster, both African American, became my first and only close friends in Alabama. They were my age. I was lonely, separated from my Loretto classmates for the first time in five years.

I caught Amy at the kitchen table sobbing, put my arm around her and asked her what was wrong. She told me about her cousin, in the church during the bombing, now in the hospital, friends arrested for protesting the bombing in Birmingham. I sat at the table and listened. I listened deeply. For the first time I remember, to an African American woman telling me the truth about her life.

She poured out her anger, her despair concerning racism, how it affected every thought, every decision, every movement she made.

Listening to her story was the first deep experience of hearing the realities of a Black friend's life, seeing the connection between her and the four little girls killed in Birmingham, then taking a small action toward becoming an antiracist. My waking up had begun on a heart level.

This was a completely different experience for me - far from the information I had from history classes in college about poverty, injustice, and racism. Or even the general call to act for social justice coming from the leader of our Loretto order, Mary Luke Tobin, as she described the Vatican II meeting she had attended in Rome that summer.

I was listening to an individual, a woman suffering, reaching my heart as no news story or statistics could.

The rest of the year, throughout news of more demonstrations, police attacks, dogs, firehoses, bombings, I listened in a new way. I insisted we talk about the issues in my English and religion classes. Some of the students from the local Maxwell Air Force base were aware of racism. But the Southern students were afraid, affected by the fears of their parents. I wanted to understand, to help, to do something, to stand up against injustice. Wasn't that part of being a real Christian, of loving one another?

I asked questions, discovered St. Jude's, the small Black Catholic high school of 150 students. I visited there, met teachers, and students. We formed an integrated baseball team, a small step toward communication between the only two Catholic high schools in the city.

I quickly learned that my Southern white students' parents were uniformly afraid to let their children take even the smallest step toward integration. I remember a female student crying because her parents wouldn't let her participate. So, our baseball games were small, often surrounded by hecklers, but we played and laughed together, peacefully. It seemed a small thing, innocent enough, but was probably the cause of my transfer at the end of the year, back to my home town of Kansas City, Missouri.

MY BEAUTIFUL PEOPLE
KANSAS CITY, MISSOURI (1964-67)

My People

The night is beautiful
So the faces of my people.

The stars are beautiful,
So the eyes of my people.

Beautiful, also, is the sun.
Beautiful, also are the souls of my people.

— Hughes

I was angry that my superiors removed me from teaching in Montgomery, without any explanation, after only one year. I had so much more work to do there. I suspected it was because of the integrated baseball team and parent complaints. I had taken a lifetime vow of obedience (in addition to the easier vows of chastity and poverty), so I wasn't to question the wisdom of my superiors, rather to see their wishes as the "will of God."

No more! I was angry. Fed up.

I questioned EVERYTHING: every dogma of the Church, every rule, every aspect of every institution in my life. Any illusion I had before Montgomery, of institutions being based on love and fairness went out the window. I had seen fear, ignorance, cruelty, and greed being the driving forces in segregation. Was that also true of the church? Where men crushed the creativity, freedom, and power of women in endless ways? These questions I could discuss openly now that I was back in my hometown, teaching with classmates who knew me so well. I explained what an awakening I had experienced in Montgomery, seeing that I had been raised here in Kansas City in similar segregation, just without the "No Colored" signs. I made new decisions too, stopped going to "confession" and told the truth instead to my sisters. I went to demonstrations against the draft, the war and racist hiring practices in schools. I was ready to act on my own conscience.

I was raised in Kansas City, Missouri, in a working-class neighborhood, a mere three blocks west of Prospect Ave, then the dividing line of Black and white homes. I don't remember any personal contacts, let alone Black neighbors, fellow students, or people at St. Mary's Catholic Church. Everything was segregated. The only place I encountered African Americans was on the public bus I took every weekday during high school. I don't remember segregation on the buses, but we did travel through poor neighborhoods, more decrepit than ours. Later, I realized I had grown up in ignorance, segregated from potential friends, playmates, teachers.

I asked my younger brothers for stories about racism in our family, and Mike said he remembered my father using the 'N' word, having negative attitudes toward Black people. Bob remembered that he had one African American boy in his class at St. Mary's in 1957. He said, "He was beaten on the playground...and I did nothing." Bobby was nine at the time, the same year the federal troops helped integrate the Little Rock Nine into Central High School in Arkansas. The same year I graduated from high school and left to become a nun. How could racism not have had a bigger impact on my life as a teenager?

If I was ignorant of racism as a teenager, I didn't need to remain ignorant now. I intensified my reading of Black authors. I dusted off copies of books from college literature courses - *Their Eyes Were Watching God* by Nora Neale Hurston and James Baldwin's *Go Tell it on a Mountain*. I studied Richard Wright, Frederick Douglas, Booker T. Washington and W.E.B DuBois, and the sermons of Dr. Martin Luther King, Jr. My fellow teachers and I also discussed articles about and by Nelson Mandela, Angela Davis and Malcolm X.

Falling in Love with my First Black Students

1964-67

During this period teaching in Kansas City, I taught my first Black students. Dyana and Shirley were dancers, as I had been throughout my high school years in that same building. I encouraged their dancing, helped them organize the school plays. Rebels too, they helped form a Black Student Union. They asked me to sponsor the club and be the chaperone of their school trip to Chicago. I listened constantly to their stories, their dreams, their struggles. One difference I noticed was our class backgrounds. I had grown up poor working class, but these students had parents who were lawyers, doctors, professionals, able to afford the tuition at a private girls' school.

I had gone to this same school on scholarship. After we became friends in class, I was invited to parties in homes of fellow white students so lavish—I had never seen anything like them. The same was probably true of my African American students now, that their homes and families reflected different class origins from mine. Yet we had so much in common - our love for the arts, for learning, for social change, and for fun.

They and other students, African American and white, helped me and Sister Maureen create Brown's - a storefront center, carved, cleaned, rescued from a poor Kansas City neighborhood. The center was envisioned as a magnet for the disadvantaged, the poor, homeless, drug addicts, anyone who needed a meal, medical care, information on social services, a place to rest and laugh. We brought our female students from Loretto, and the Christian Brothers from De La Salle nearby brought their guys to tear out old walls and trash, scrub, erect plasterboard, paint, decorate. Once the electricity and bathrooms functioned well enough, we welcomed people from the streets every weekend. All of the nuns and brothers involved were also full-time teachers, so we integrated the work at Browns into our classes, both by discussing the issue of poverty and allowing the students to experience it first hand.

Sr. David Maureen (or Maureen Smith), my good friend who created Brown's, the storefront in KC, MO. Kansas City Star, c.1966

One of my best friends, Christian Brother David Darst, taught me and his students about the relationship of poverty to war. He also wrote amazing poetry describing his students who died in Vietnam. He, Maureen, Judith, all of us young nuns, priests and brothers became activists against racism, poverty, war, and oppression. Several went to Selma for the march with Martin Luther King. I longed to join them, but permission was denied by my superiors. I deeply resented that decision. But they could not stop our radicalization, our teaching students the truth.

Nor could anyone stop us from loving one another, our students, and the poor we served. David was filled with energy, life, a new perspective on almost everything, one of the most brilliant teachers I've known. His students adored his whimsical absorption in a comic book, his way with words - "My heart's running to catch the sunshine."

He and other inspiring young Christian Brothers and Jesuit priests at Rockhurst High School also became models for my own brother Bob, who was a high school student while I taught at Loretto. He was attracted to visiting me at the all-girls' school, of course, and worked with my students at Brown's. What a thrill to have my own baby brother dishing out soup at my side, seeing a new part of the city and life.

My First African American Teacher

1965

In the summer of 1965, I won a scholarship to attend classes at St. Thomas College in St. Paul, MN. I had always taken year-round classes since I entered the Sisters of Loretto. Constant graduate study expanded my teaching credentials from the five areas of my Life-Time Teaching Certificate (English, History, Education, French and Latin) to yet more areas I could teach..

Hank Parker walked into our classroom at St. Thomas on that first morning of Advanced Rhetoric class. He was tall, slim, with a touch of grey in his short afro. His features sharp, the bones of his face strong, his smooth skin deep brown. I had not researched him before the class, so I was surprised to see my first African American professor.

The surprises were just beginning. He had the entire class entranced with his soft, compelling tone - "Welcome to the magic of words." He probably had my heart in his hands from that day. He challenged our minds, stretched our hearts and voices. We wrote, edited, stood in front of the other students regularly, stumbled, straightened, did whatever possible to please him.

I met with him privately, something forbidden just two years earlier, before final vows. It is probably still discouraged for women with vows of chastity to meet privately with any man. I rationalized that I needed help with my next speech. Made an appointment, waited nervously in the hall, heard his laugh through the door. The student meeting with him opened the door to leave, Dr. Parker followed him, leaned out into the hallway, and said, "Sister Joann, please come in." Hank Parker was the first live, official Black professor I remember. His elegance, intelligence and excellent teaching still lives in me.

Black Teachers! Galore!

However, Dr. Parker wasn't the first African American to open my mind and heart to the realities of racism. My religious order is one of the most progressive ever, so professors of history and English at Webster University had introduced me in the early sixties to Ralph Ellison, Langston Hughes, and many other authors.

Now actively involved in the Civil Rights Movement in my hometown, I read these authors and new voices such as Bobby Seale and Huey Newton with an opened heart. It wouldn't be until 1969 that I was able to visit Black Panther Party breakfast programs, schools, and rallies around the country. But my political views about oppressed people standing up, taking up arms to defend themselves, and fighting back struggled inside with my deep commitment to non-violence. I had been able to understand the Vietnamese people arming themselves against US bombs. I understood the Panthers legally arming themselves against police brutality and injustice. But my heart resisted the notion of ever picking up a gun myself or harming anyone as an effective way to change our society. I wanted to believe that Gandhi's ahimsa and Martin Luther King's soul force were more powerful weapons than any guns or bombs.

BECOMING AN ALLY TO BLACK POWER

April 4, 2017

Bobby Seale, co-founder of the Black Panther Party answered questions after his talk at the University of Washington on the anniversary of Martin Luther King's assassination.

"Q: What do you think about white allies in the fight for black liberation?"

Seale: *"Good. Just as people in the Underground Railroad had white allies who ran the Underground Railroad locations, you know, yes to that extent, yes. It's not just about white allies; it's about progressive thinking allies who are truly representative to being opposed to that vicious institution of human slavery. Those are the kind of allies you need whether they are black, white, blue, yellow, green, or polka dot. Those are the true* *allies you need. Look, we said power to the people. It's about all the people. When you talk about constitutional and democratic rights, those rights are not just for black folks."*

— BOBBY SEALE

How can I become a good ally? A real Antiracist? Listen, connect with African Americans and act in effective ways to stop injustice? Was I beginning to act more courageously and more publicly by 1967?

In the summer of 1967, I was traveling by train to a new city, a new teaching assignment. Nerinx Hall HS was just blocks from Webster University, and I had done student teaching there. I had no desire to live again under the restrictions of the large community center where I had lived during my college years. So, two other sisters and I arranged to live above a garage behind the convent of an elementary school in the St. Louis inner city, a predominantly African American area. We sometimes ate with the sisters, but led a fairly independent lifestyle, driving our used car daily to teach in Webster Groves, the conservative white suburb.

Long, Hot Summer of 1967

1967 is referred to as the "long, hot summer" of riots in 159 cities, one of the worst in Newark, forty-seven miles from the college. Twenty-six people killed, 1500 injured and at least that many arrested. Across the river, the rioting spilled into Manhattan in the form of protests and 'happenings' we students organized. I remember also working in a predominantly African American community center in Bridgeport, CT that summer, listening to stories of children who suffered all their lives from poverty, hunger, poor education, fear of police.

That summer I also began an interdisciplinary graduate program at Manhattanville in White Plains, NY, 30 miles from NYC where we traveled weekly for lectures, museums, and other forms of learning. This was a two-year experience that also greatly broadened my perspective on racism, art, and LIFE!

This was the summer we "ditched the habit." Officially the change didn't happen until shortly before school opened. Overnight we went from a full, black habit and veil covering all our hair to "anything we wished to wear." This had been a change that we younger nuns had lobbied for, hoping it would decrease the obstacles between us and the people we served..

Internal Breaks with Old Ways of Thinking and Living

The external change in clothing was minor compared to the profound internal changes I experienced. My theological search and growing political awareness of the role of the Catholic Church in world poverty and complicity with war and oppression led me to the decision to distance myself from the hierarchical church. I remained a Sister of Loretto, deeply committed to the spiritual and humanitarian values of love, self-sacrifice for others and non-violent action. But the Catholic Church's vast land holdings in South America, complicity with the Nazis in WWII, and failure to condemn the war in Vietnam or the actions of Israel against the Palestinians disgusted me. I no longer believed in many of the basic teachings of the Church on papal infallibility, the one true church, the virgin birth, the teachings on hell, contraception, and divorce. I knew too much about how these teachings harmed the lives of people I worked with and loved, especially poor Catholics, including my own mother.

As a budding feminist, I knew that Loretto women were far better qualified than most men in the church to teach, heal, and spread the message of love. We owned and operated two colleges, dozens of high schools, and hundreds of elementary schools – with more interference than assistance from the hierarchical, patriarchal church. I started my slow separation from the Church by confessing my doubts to fellow Lorettos instead of priests, baring my soul, opening my heart to their challenges to be more courageous and honest. I wasn't any angel, still struggling with my demons of fear (rooted in our family problems), mistrust, selfishness, people-pleasing, pride, intellectual arrogance, rebellion and lust for respect and admiration. But I could be more open with my sisters who observed my behavior and attitude every day than whispering to a male priest who didn't know me. Vatican II also urged us to be more collegial and democratic in our efforts at spiritual growth, no longer relying primarily on "superiors" and other official authority figures.

These changes came slowly, and my friends and I in the order debated them constantly. The experience of our sisters in Latin American missions awakened us to the necessity for true Christians to be involved in movements for social justice. Good friends of mine, Sisters of Loretto in Chile, Peru, El Salvador, Nicaragua, and Bolivia, were caught in revolutionary actions because they worked with and loved the poor in those countries. Families they had visited, counseled, and taught were kidnapped and killed by military governments supported by U.S. funds. Bodies of friends who had been tortured were left on the doorsteps of their family homes. Thousands of children in our schools received insufficient food and medical care. Women were trapped by centuries of inhumane restrictions on their freedom to be full human beings. Sisters and priests pleaded with the Catholic bishops to stop the wealthy from exploiting and killing the poor. They told us of the intransigency of the institutional church, the same resistance we experienced in the US when we worked directly with the poor, the civil rights movement and the anti-war movement.

I was particularly impressed by the changes I witnessed in people like my friend Penny, now my roommate. I had never heard her express any views about politics or "liberation theology" until she returned from Latin America. She had been profoundly changed by seeing the level of poverty of the children she taught, horrified at fathers being carried off by the government for non-payment of taxes, impatient with the hierarchical church members who ignored the pleas of their people for help with children sick and starving. She looked the same, except for her grey robes, but her spirit had been transformed by compassion for her students and their families in Bolivia. She was now willing to stand up to governments and bishops to get medicine, food, and schools for her children. She made me think deeply about the educational theories of Paolo Freire and the priests who had actually joined liberation organizations or taken up arms against dictatorships in Latin America. Penny was a friend, a revolutionary to the core, a woman who would eventually become my strongest supporter and ally in my own actions against the U.S. government.

Vatican II directives urged us to act based on our consciences, to be bold in making changes in the church to fulfill our mission to serve the poor, to live the teachings of the New Testament. Since our own Sister Luke Tobin had been the sole woman invited to attend Vatican II as the President of the Association of Women Religious in the US, she eagerly brought us first-hand information and continued to instigate debate on many issues. Our order did become more democratic, more committed to social justice and open to deep changes in rules, liturgy, and customs.

These revolutionary changes the summer before my new teaching assignment in St. Louis affected my teaching at Nerinx. I knew that I faced a more conservative, suburban, and naïve group of girls than I had in urban Kansas City Most were white and had never been "down in the inner city." Few had ever met someone who had been as poor as I had been growing up, let alone poor and Black.

Protest against the Pruitt-Igo projects in St. Louis

On field trips in our religion classes, I took them to Pruit-Igo, a horrible government-built slum high-rise. I am still convinced that many middle-class white Americans don't truly understand what poverty is because they don't see it. In St. Louis, people could drive by slums full of suffering on their way to work downtown. In the type of religion classes my fellow sisters and the Christian Brothers developed in Kansas City, we did service projects taking young suburbanites to the inner city to help deliver food, medical and social services to the poor. We were probably awkward in our attempts to be useful, but at least the students came back with a deeper awareness of poverty, social injustice, racism and the oppression of women and children.

We got to know the individuals, the children and their families who lived lives of poverty and racial discrimination our students could hardly imagine. Students and teachers came to deeply respect the courage, resilience and creativity of single mothers raising their children with almost no resources. In weekend retreats, we used the teaching methods of Paulo Freire's *Pedagogy of the Oppressed* to awaken compassion, empowerment, and commitment to social change. I also learned that poor people saw no benefit in us becoming poor with them. They wanted freedom, equality, and change.

Our Friends, the Black Liberators

It was while living on Taylor Street in St. Louis that we became friends with the leaders of the Black Liberators, founded in the spring of 1968 after the murder of Dr. Martin Luther King, Jr. They were an offshoot of the Black Panther Party, founded two years earlier in Oakland, CA. Trust was slow in coming, but eventually Leon Dent and Charles Koen became guests for dinner at the Taylor St. convent. The older nuns probably saw the young black men as grown versions of the kids they loved and taught every day. They didn't necessarily associate them with the stories of the Black Panther Party, CORE or SNCC they heard on the news. We listened to their histories of racial discrimination in Southern Illinois where Koen was raised. We heard the difficulties for young Black men to support families, to recover from physical and psychological traumas in Vietnam, to stay out of prison, to kick drug habits, and to survive police brutality.

Nuns March to Urge Release of Black Liberators

One day, we were called to do more than merely listen to stories when Charles and Leon were arrested on an afternoon in December 1968 for "insufficiently lighted license plates." They were taken into the local jail and beaten mercilessly by nine policemen. Even though the two young Black men had broken hands, cuts and bruises about their heads, shoulders and eyes and bruised ribs, the police claimed they attacked police officers in the jail. I knew the police were lying. Leon, Charles, and my other Black Liberator friends were not stupid people, not suicidal either. We nuns received their "one phone call," called lawyers, the press, and our network of religious activists. Within a day, fifty nuns marched to the St Louis police headquarters and demanded their release and an audience with the chief of police. Both of our demands were met, since we took the press along and the action appeared on the nightly news. We took the two young men to the hospital for treatment, and one of them went underground before their trial.

My first batch of hate mail poured into the Taylor St. convent and Nerinx Hall H.S., following coverage in the local St. Louis Post-Dispatch and television stations. I had grown up in a totally segregated society but had not personally been the recipient of such pure hatred and racist venom. Doctor Winterer from Webster Groves sent a picture from the St. Louis Post-Dispatch with another picture of two young African American men beaten by police in the street. His letter said, "Here you are, you poor misguided soul—another group of hoodlums and animals for you to defend." Others sent articles like the "Dan Smoot Report" which accused civil rights activists of being "manipulated by sinister forces to do the job of the communist party: to tear American Society apart and destroy constitutional government." He listed prominent Americans such as Thurgood Marshall, Roy Wilkins, and Ralph Bunche as "communist fronts."

Another included an article stating that three-fourths of teachers in East St. Louis public schools carry firearms. A protest by religious women against the brutal beating of two young Black men in a police station touched deep fears of racial equality and prompted the American right to identify our outrage at police brutality with accusations of being Communist and threats of violence. There was also positive support from our sisters, from some students and community activists. But clearly, we had a great deal of work to do to educate people about the effects of poverty, racism and war.

An Encounter with a Black Liberator

One of the nuns at the elementary school, Dianne, developed a relationship with one of the Black Liberators that became more than just friendship. She was twenty-five, the same age as this dynamic young man. They often sat at our large dining room table, discussing his childhood in Cairo, Illinois. Dianne's friend was a vivid storyteller, describing his seven siblings in one bed, his father in jail, mother working two jobs, and encounters with police. One night over wine, their conversation extended into the early hours of the morning, after the rest of us had gone to bed.

Later that week, after the arrest of Leon and Charles happened, the house mobilized to organize the demonstration and the press banged at our convent door. The Liberator's storefront was firebombed, and several of our friends had to disappear into the underground or face arrest and imprisonment. Dianne's young man was among those who had to leave town for good, facing charges he knew were false.

Several months later, Dianne found she was pregnant. One night together, and now pregnant! The father of her child gone from her life, a wanted man, never knowing he had become a father.

She decided to leave the order, continue the pregnancy, raise the baby herself. Her family disowned her and refused to acknowledge an African American granddaughter.

Ironically we both met again in California, less than two years later, when I was in hiding from the FBI, pregnant with my son, facing thirty-five years in federal prison, fearful the government would take my baby. Her daughter was a beautiful little girl.

ACTION AGAINST WAR AND RACISM

1967-69

"The Black Power advocates are disenchanted with the inconsistencies in the militaristic posture of our government. Over the past decade they have seen America applauding nonviolence whenever the Negroes have practiced it. They have watched it being praised in the sit-in movements of 1960, in the Freedom Riots of 1961, in the Albany movement of 1962, in the Birmingham movement of 1963 and in the Selma movement of 1965. But then these same black young men and women have watched as America sends black young men to burn Vietnamese with napalm, to slaughter men, women, and children; and they wonder what kind of nation applauds nonviolence whenever Negroes face white people in the streets of the United State but then applauds violence and burning and death when these same Negroes are sent to the fields of Vietnam."

— MARTIN LUTHER KING JR, 1957

Martin Luther King called out the hypocrisy of the US government urging non-violence in the Civil Rights Movement but forcing an inordinate number of Black soldiers to murder Vietnamese people and die in its name. He organized a rally of 125,000 in protest against the war. SNCC had issued statements against the Vietnam War as early as 1965, declaring that Black people should not "fight in Vietnam for the white man's freedom, until all the Negro people are free in Mississippi."

Huge changes happened in the movement during 1967-68, including peace-makers like Dan Berrigan speaking out against white supremacy and African American leaders in the Civil Rights movement speaking out against the war in Vietnam.

Martin Luther King and Thich Nhat Hanh (one of the only photos taken of them together - in 1966, I believe, when MLK nominated TNH for the Nobel Peace Prize).

I also attended a talk by Thich Nhat Hanh where he described the horrors of napalm, bombing and the deaths of family and friends. His demeanor in responding to a heckler to "go back to Vietnam" touched my heart. This incident is described in the introduction by Jim Forrest to Thich Nhat Hanh's book *The Miracle of Mindfulness* which I discovered years later :

"There was one evening when Nhat Hanh awoke not understanding the rage of one American. Nhat Hanh had been talking in the auditorium of a wealthy Christian church in a St. Louis suburb. As always, he emphasized the need for Americans to stop their bombing and killing in his country. There had been questions and answers when a large man stood up and spoke with searing scorn of the 'supposed compassion' of 'this Mr. Hanh.'

'If you care so much about your people, Mr. Hanh, why are you here? If you care so much for the people who are wounded, why don't you spend your time with them?'

When he finished, I looked toward Nhat Hanh in bewilderment. What could he—or anyone—say? The spirit of the war itself had suddenly filled the room, and it seemed hard to breathe.

There was a silence. Then Nhat Hanh began to speak—quietly, with deep calm, indeed with a sense of personal caring for the man who had just damned him. The words seemed like rain falling on fire. 'If you want the tree to grow,' he said, 'it won't help to water the leaves. You have to water the roots. Many of the roots of the war are here, in your country. To help the people who are to be bombed, to try to protect them from this suffering, I have to come here.'

The atmosphere in the room was transformed. In the man's fury we had experienced our own furies; we had seen the world as through a bomb bay. In Nhat Hanh's response we had experienced an alternate possibility: the possibility (here brought to Christians by a Buddhist and to Americans by an 'enemy') of overcoming hatred with love, of breaking the seemingly endless chain reaction of violence throughout human history." (Hanh, 2016).

By this time I had participated in numerous draft and anti-war demonstrations, but on May 17, 1968, when my friend David Darst burned draft files with the Catonsville Nine, my heart told me I had to go further. I participated in organizing retreats for actions, saw police attack peaceful demonstrators at the Chicago Democratic Convention. I helped organize the Milwaukee 14 draft action, attended the Catonsville 9 trial. We held protests around the country against Dow Chemical's production of napalm, nerve gas and defoliants, which were killing hundreds of thousands of Vietnamese people, in addition to US soldiers spraying Agent Orange. With Thich Nhat Hahn's words echoing in my mind, I decided to participate in the DC-9 action against Dow Chemical's profiting from murder.

Darst (right) with fellow defendant Dan Berrigan. been worth it. Just the publicity that have had a young man

Finally, after secret meetings on the East coast and careful planning on untapped pay phones, we had two actions planned in Washington, D.C. for March,1969. Those of us who had committed to participation in the action were aware we faced decades in jail and possible death. The police might overreact to our burglary of the Dow Chemical lobbying office and the draft board in D.C. I was ready. It was one of the most difficult decisions of my life, but I felt it was the next necessary non-violent step against this unjust and brutal war, against a racist system. I was ready to give my life for my country, for its people, its true democratic principles and for the people of Vietnam.

Early on Saturday morning, March 22, 1969, we gathered to break into the Dow office. None of the nine of us lived in D.C.; we traveled secretly from Cleveland, New York, St. Louis, San Francisco and Detroit. Others thoroughly cased the building; it had few workers on Saturdays and the Dow office was closed. The priests wore their Roman collars. We could have signed in "Dow Chemical" with the guard downstairs, we were so confident that we would not be disturbed until we had finished our work. We took the elevator to the fifth floor and used a crowbar on the outside door. We brought appropriate tools for "breaking and entering" and "destruction of property," two of the charges against us. My small claim to fame would be becoming the first nun in the US to commit federal felonies. Five of them!

Once inside, Catherine Melville and I proceeded to look through the files for damaging evidence of Dow's involvement in the war in Vietnam, while Mike Slaski took care of smashing some of the equipment. Two others carefully taped the windows before breaking them so that the glass would fall inside the office. We had several people posted on the ground to keep pedestrians from walking past when the glass broke and to alert reporters to capture the picture of the files flowing from the Dow Chemical windows. We were committed to protesting in a non-violent way. Two others decorated the walls with our slogans against the war, written in our own blood.

I found a "Five year plan" in which Dow Chemical projected its profit from napalm, nerve gas and defoliants until 1974. They planned to continue to make millions from the death and destruction of the people of Vietnam. The cold figures on the white paper, the statistical charts were death sentences for hundreds of thousands of Vietnamese people and American soldiers. We meant to expose their true nature as weapons of mass destruction. These files were added to the others flowing down to K Street below. Our colleagues retrieved them and handed them to the press. Exposés would soon appear in the Washington Post and New York Times.

AP photo, Kansas City Star, 1969

This was the first action of the Catholic Left that focused on the role of US corporations in the war, demonstrating that the war in Vietnam was by nature a war of imperialism. We showed proof by publishing the "Five Year Plan" and other documents. The war was not primarily about "stopping the spread of communism" or other government propaganda. It was a war of expanding US power, economic and political domination over other peoples and nations. We took a step further in our attack against the morality of the war to a more revolutionary analysis of class, race and imperialism.

Soon several policemen barged into the Dow office, guns drawn and arrested us. We waited for them, knowing the consequences. We could have easily escaped, as did many people in future actions. But part of the point of our action was to "stand there," to take responsibility for what we had done, as religious leaders with pristine records, to be able to speak in court and to the press and to those who knew us well as respected members of five different communities around the country.

We were handcuffed, gratefully not shot by nervous police and hauled off to D.C. Women's Detention Center and the D.C. Jail.

A MINORITY IN JAIL

"Why do we take prison for granted? While a relatively small proportion of the populations ever directly experienced life inside prison, this is not true in poor black and Latino communities…It is difficult to imagine life without prisons. At the same time, there is reluctance to face the realities hidden within them, a fear of thinking about what happens inside them. Thus, the prison is present in our lives and, at the same time, it is absent from our lives."

— ANGELA DAVIS

March 22, 1969

I had never been handcuffed, strip-searched, or poked by guards in private areas of my body, finger-printed, photographed with a number around my neck. No one had even hugged me without my permission for years. I was a nun! Though no one in the D.C. Jail could tell I was a nun just by looking at me. They saw me only as a law-breaker, a felon, part of a vast number of criminals in the system.

Cathy and I still felt both relief and an adrenaline high at succeeding in our mission. But after the booking, we began to experience exhaustion at the sleepless nights observing the draft board building the nights before our action. Finally we were led, dressed in too-large prison cotton, into the general population dayroom of the D.C. Women's Detention Center.

There were a couple of hefty women near the door and a crowd behind them gathered to check out these two unusual white prisoners. One of the heaviest women began making clicking sounds with her lips and moved closer to me, whispering that she needed a new roommate. I picked up on the signal, and with a smile and shrug, trying to indicate some regret in having to pass up a great offer, indicated Cathy with my thumb and said, "I'm with her." Everyone laughed. It diffused the immediate "introduction" tension and got us into our bunk beds for the first night.

This was not my first time living with Black people. The nuns from Kerala lived with us for years at the Motherhouse in dorms and at the House of Studies, missing their families in India. I traveled with my Elegant Eight, my African American students in the Kansas City Black Student Union, to Chicago, and loved them like a substitute mother.

But now we were naked in showers, sleeping together, fellow inmates, some upset, stumbling into the dayroom drunk, high, beaten, sharing our stories without barriers. It was definitely my first experience of living as an ethnic minority in an all-Black community. Of course, this wasn't a 'community' of choice. The guards, administrators, lawyers, keepers of the keys were all white. But, except for Cathy and me for those ten days, all the residents were African American.

In *My Grandmother's Hands* by Resmaa Menakem, he notes

> "One aspect of white-body supremacy involves seeing 'whites' as the norm standard for human, and people of color as a deviation from that norm…an actress becomes a black actress, and so on... This everyday form of white-body supremacy is in the air we breathe, the water we drink, and the culture we share. We literally cannot avoid it. It is part of the operating system and organizing structure of American culture. It's always functioning in the background, often invisibly, in our institutions, our relationships and our interactions."
>
> — MENAKEM

D.C. Women's Detention Center, 1969

By the next morning, word had spread throughout the detention center that I was a nun, Cathy an ex-nun/revolutionary from Guatemala and that we had been arrested for five federal felonies.

They had never heard of women trying to get arrested, standing around waiting for the cops to show up! Were we nuts?

The story was on the front page of the Washington Post, all over the television news. So, the minute we re-entered the dayroom, we were surrounded with questions.

"Why'd you stand there?"

"Why didn't you run?"

"Did you really use your own blood?"

"Why Dow Chemical?"

We plopped down on the rusty chairs and held our first informal press conference.

"Yes it was our own blood. A nurse drew it for us, and we brought it inside the office in small bottles. We wanted to remind Dow that their files selling napalm caused deaths of real people - Vietnamese children and US soldiers."

"Yeah, my son's there."

"Well, we meant to also destroy all the draft records for D.C. too, but that action got stopped. We hope your son comes home safely. We want all US soldiers to come home. And we want the draft to stop!"

Then we asked for names, asked about the women's families, whether they got to have visitors, how their children survived without them.

One evening, I spent more time getting to know Keisha:

"I've been in this fuckin' hole 16 months... they're not supposed to keep anyone longer than a year. Nothin' to do, nothin' to read, no recreation, can't get outdoors. I haven't been outside at all, except once to see a doctor. The hole? The hole is hell - 'specially for girl's goin' through cold turkey. They turned the water off in one girl's cell for two days while she was kickin'. No medicine, no one comin' round, no air. People are put in the hole for all kinds of things - sittin' on the stairs, talkin' back, bein' sick. Addicts aren't treated like humans. It's a sickness, these drugs, and they need treatment. I shoot because I'm depressed."

After talking to Keisha, I gave her a hug, then slipped back into the cell with some paper towels I'd swiped and a small pencil one of the inmates had found for me. Being without paper and pen was harder for me than not having a toothbrush for those weeks or not eating the whole time we were there (we fasted in protest at the conditions). I longed to jot down some of the conversations, the lilt of tone, the slang. I still have that hand-towel journal, the beginning of a fifty-year habit, not wanting to miss any moment of this intense experience of becoming a criminal, of living as a minority in the prison culture.

My first experience in the D.C. jail would end within a couple of weeks, even though I was told by lawyers I faced thirty-five possible years in prison. I was interested in learning as much as possible about jail, courts and prison life.

For most of the Black women here, jail was a way of life. Some were also first-timers, but many had been through the prison system in an endless cycle of poverty, unemployment, domestic abuse, homelessness, illness, addiction, and the unreliability of the welfare and health care systems. Hearing their stories and trying to take notes on them became as much a daily routine as writing letters to superiors, my principal, supporters and family.

Cecilia seemed so young and sweet - and scared. Her dress was a little girls size and showed that she was at least five months pregnant. Her smile was ready, but she cried a lot when she thought about her husband. He was in the hospital suffering from a knife wound. She had stabbed him in self-defense and waited outside the hospital in a detective's car to hear about his condition. Then she heard nothing more about him for a day and a half of waiting, processing, finger-printing, stripping, questioning, confiscation of personal belongings, isolation, and trying to sleep next to a blaring television. The next day brought twelve more hours of waiting in the bullpen - no word of her husband, no lawyer, no money for bail, no hope. Her crying rarely stopped.

Frances was the mother of eleven, always smiling in her gentle good humor, her thoughtfulness and lack of criticism at daily indignities. She had short-cropped hair and a round face with wide-open eyes. She had a childlike wonder listening to another woman describing her drug addiction. "I don't think I could make my children go hungry for the sake of a kick for myself." We regretted seeing her leave but were happy for her. When she laughed, her belly - the largest part of her body - wiggled with delight. I never heard her mention why she had been arrested.

Gloria, I liked on sight. She talked so openly about her life, her interests, hang-ups, but in a way that gave others space too. She wasn't pushy. She was very intelligent, had worked for the US government, and traveled. She mentioned her children often, and loved them. She was a charmer, but not in a manipulative way, just lovely.

I made gratitude lists in my paper towel journal, for these women who were kind to us newcomers. I was grateful for sheets and blankets, the radio in the dayroom (but not the television blaring 24 hours a day!). Grateful an inmate had warned us about crabs and unique ways to get rid of them. I wrote my feelings, which were changing hourly with the fasting making everything sharp and real.

Hearing so many stories of the women who knew the D.C. jail well, Cathy and I decided to fast in protest against the war and the conditions in the jail. It was a wise thing to do anyway just to avoid the horrible food, but we knew that it could be a powerful method of resistance too. So we took fluids, water and coffee, but asked that trays of food be sent back. On the third day, after arraignment, the guards noticed that we were not eating. They notified the administrators of the jail who threatened to force eggs down our noses with tubes if we didn't at least take dietary supplements. We compromised and drank those, but refused solid food during our entire stay.

For the first several days, fasting was difficult, but once my stomach adjusted, my mind started feeling lighter and clearer. I had fasted during Lent in the early convent days, but had never gone this long without any solid food. I thought of the women there who told us how hard it was to find money for food for their children, the desperate lengths necessary to find a few dollars. So, they had more questions about how we were feeling, why we were doing this, would it change anything?

"You know, you girls are different, don't you? That you'll get out, that there are people out there supporting you, that your names are on the front page of the paper," said Gloria. "I would never pass up a meal."

"You're right. We have lots of support. My order isn't even taking away my teaching job. We'll probably be declared indigent and get out on bond, our lawyers say. We have some good court-appointed people. I suppose since we're all in this jail together right now, we can use those privileges to fight for equality for all of us. It's not right that you have terrible food, no books in the library, no recreation or chance to get outdoors. You shouldn't be thrown in the 'hole' for nothing. There shouldn't BE a 'hole'! We'll be out in a few days. But since we're facing long prison sentences, we'd better keep fighting for justice for all of us!"

At that moment, we heard voices hollering our names outside the window, went to look out the grimy glass and saw a large candlelight vigil forming. I recognized friends' voices singing "We Shall Overcome" and "I get by with a little help from my friends." Posters announced, "We're fasting with you!" And "Abolish prisons!"

Gloria's honesty, "telling me like it was," sent me back to my cell to write more about white privilege. I had a lot to learn about the everyday injustices of racism, the advantages I had as a white woman, even as a felon.

MY WHITE PRIVILEGE 2020

I've never liked being categorized as "white."

What's white?

An absence of color, melanin, jazz, laughter, rhythm? I probably never even heard the term growing up. I knew I was Irish. I was Catholic and was taught to defend my faith to the death like Maria Goretti, who was stabbed to death rather than give up her virginity. I should avoid "non-Catholics," who might endanger my faith (although my best friend from age four had a Protestant parent). I don't think I met a Jewish person until my mid-20s. Religious differences were made very clear to me.

I felt angry at my second class status as a woman and vowed one day at age seven, while dusting the legs of the dining room table, to never, ever get married. I decided that day I would never voluntarily become the slave of some husband who drank and slept on the couch while I worked.

I didn't really feel the impact of class differences until high school. Other kids in my Catholic grade school were also poor working class. Our church was so pitiful that we never could afford to build a real church building and had services in the stone foundation. I was shocked to meet girls in my private high school who owned their own cars. Our family had never been able to afford a car, except for one six-month period of time before my father lost his job in the flour mill and we kicked him out of the house for good. That separation was a dark secret I could never share with any of my fancy high school friends. My prom dress was a hand-me-down from an aunt, most of my clothes sewn by my mother. I started saving money for piano lessons from babysitting neighbors at age eight. I worked from then until almost sixty-seven. I don't remember anyone in our extended family "retiring." They just worked til they died. I definitely felt our family was from a different world than my wealthy classmates. But we wore uniforms, so my clothes didn't usually give away my inferior status. None of them were ever invited to our home, however.

All my childhood, my white privilege was an unknown reality to me out of sheer ignorance and segregation from people who had less privilege and equal rights because of the color of their skin. I didn't know any Black people then, hadn't yet visited their homes, studied under them, read their books, become friends.

Montgomery, Alabama radically changed my consciousness of white privilege. It was quite clear there that African Americans suffered great injustice from the legacy of slavery. Governor George Wallace protected Jim Crow segregation with a vengeance by allowing police to use attack dogs and firehoses on protesters. In Alabama, white privilege was visible - little girls firebombed in the Birmingham church, Rosa Parks sitting in the white section of the bus, Martin Luther King, Jr. leading the Selma March. Living there a year had given me new eyes to see my own upbringing and privileges in Kansas City, Missouri. I could no longer turn back or deny the advantages in my life, that I was able through education and connection with a group of religious women, to climb out of poverty into the college-educated middle class.

While I suffered from segregation, from the lack of experience of having African American friends in my childhood, my Black neighbors suffered real deprivation from unequal housing, jobs, education, healthcare and political power.

Once my eyes began to open to white supremacy, first in college theoretically, then on my first teaching assignment in Montgomery on a deep gut level, I could never unsee what was so clear. This experience radicalized me, set me on a journey to see, learn, fight for and stand up for racial justice. It is still helping me look more deeply at my own blindness, to understand how my words and actions still carry unconscious prejudice.

White privilege, seeing one's color as the norm is an illusion, a form of blindness. Those who promote color-blindness are simply building another wall of denial to the reality of an unjust, unequal system based on racism. I can see and articulate this truth now, with the insights of African American proponents of antiracism. Today I choose again to keep my eyes open, to stand against our unjust system as an antiracist. I still have much to learn in this process and hope to remain teachable to any who detect in my words or actions that deep white supremacist system in which I was raised.

In *How to be an Antiracist*, Ibram X. Kendi states, "But for all of that life-shaping power, race is a mirage, which doesn't lessen its force. We are what we see ourselves as, whether what we see exists or not. We are what people see us as, whether what they see exists or not. What people see in themselves and others has meaning and manifests itself in ideas and actions and policies, even if what they are seeing is an illusion. Race is a mirage but one that we do well to see, while never forgetting it is a mirage, never forgetting that it's the powerful light of racist power that makes the mirage. (Kendi, 2019, p. 37).

SPEAKING OUT AGAINST WAR, RACISM, CORPORATE KILLING

Backlash

2020

In early November, hundreds of people rallied in D.C. to protest the outcome of the presidential elections. Some must believe that election fraud existed. Were they angry and disappointed that their leader would no longer have the power to disregard the Covid pandemic, fuel racist hatred and defend white supremacy in our country? Or were they simply afraid of losing power, privilege, their jobs, homes, status? I want to understand, to listen to their views and feelings also. I admit that it is difficult and takes all the training I have since received in non-judgment and compassion to listen and hope to understand better.

The intransigence, anger and violence of the protest took me back emotionally to the week I returned from the D.C. jail to face people who disagreed with my action against Dow Chemical. I need to listen, since there are millions of my fellow-Americans who seem to think, feel, vote and act very differently from me. I know in my heart that there are no opposites, them and us. We are one people and must find common ground if we are to survive.

April, 1969

St. Louis U speech

I returned to Nerinx Hall HS, surrounded by hostile white parents, students and lay teachers, screaming at me. I tried to respond but couldn't be heard in that setting and could barely hear the words behind the spittle and red faces. About two-hundred fifty parents met in the school auditorium on April 8, 1969 determined to keep me from returning to the classroom the next day.

In jail, I had time to further articulate and write my message about the action to my principal, Sr. Helen Jean and others. The language seems abstract to me now -"Our action is a confrontation with all American corporations which hide their exploitation of people under the sterile, legal, and moral guise of free enterprise." But I also wrote more personally to this woman, also my former novice mistress, who had to defend me to irate parents - "There were so many times when I wanted to speak to you more directly about the racism, the selfishness which can confine us to narrow views of life if we do not search constantly for wider views of man, society, ourselves, and refuse to allow dullness and fear to control our decisions and our lifestyles. Schools must be challenged with the urgency of burning children, starving families in our city, devastated countries which our country bombs. If you were dying, I would want to save you, regardless of the cost to me in terms of job, position, respect or even a criminal record."

Reporters showed up at the school, the convent and numerous press conferences. In just a few weeks, I had become a celebrity, on the front page of several national newspapers, the subject of articles, letters to editors and newscasts. I had to learn to articulate my message about war, racism, poverty and the profit Dow was making from suffering and war. I learned quickly to speak in soundbites, briefly, clearly, while keeping my calm, not letting antagonism stir me to making remarks that could not be erased. I made mistakes, tried to learn from them.

"We refuse to cooperate with the war machine"

"Dow can restore its files, but it can't restore one life or limb of a child they have destroyed by napalm."

"Yes, this is a crusade - against a system that values property over human life."

"Some property doesn't have a right to exist - like slums, napalm, and the Selective Service draft files."

Questioned about our action causing chaos, I replied, "The DC-9 action will not incite anarchy. We already live in chaos and mass murder. We want to meet chaos with a human response."

I echoed similar defenses of non-violent actions, similar to ours, from my teachers - Gandhi, Martin Luther King, Malcolm X, Dorothy Day and John Lewis.

It Took a VILLAGE of Support.

This one individual white woman-body did say YES to committing the DC-9 action, but I was never alone in that action or the statement it was meant to make. I was called "weird," "a sinner," "criminal," "vandal," "irresponsible," "arrogant."

Some of those terms remind me of the bad apple syndrome being touted now with brutal police officers. But whatever my individual failures or characteristics, I was no more a lone actor than are cops who kill African Americans today. I was the product of a world-wide resistance movement against the white supremacist system and against the Dow Chemical Company's "right" to make napalm to kill people of color.

Re-reading the statement we made to the press during the action, and especially the statements of the Sisters of Loretto defending my right to take the action, I'm amazed at the anti-imperialist analysis in both.

"You corporations, who under the cover of stockholders and executive anonymity, exploit, deprive, dehumanize and kill in search of profit (DC-9 pamphlet quote)."

The DC-9 was different from previous anti-war actions in that it was the first action that planned to combine burning draft files with destroying corporate napalm files. Unfortunately the draft board part of our action was blocked by informers and the removal of the files the night before that part of the action. We did destroy Dow Chemical property, files, poured blood, waited to be arrested in the tradition of thousands of non-violent protestors against Jim Crow laws. And, though we were prepared to be beaten or shot, that didn't happen to a group of white destroyers of property. I don't have the physical courage that John Lewis demonstrated in over forty arrests and numberless beatings and serious injuries.

However radical our statement against capitalism itself, perhaps more noteworthy are the references to racism in the statements of the Sisters of Loretto who stood with me as one of their own, raised and educated from childhood by their values.

In her letter to the Board and Sisters at Nerinx, Sister Luke Tobin, our Mother General, said:

"If we as sisters have to suffer because of the words and deeds by which we attempt to assist our neighbors in need, especially the victims of racism, poverty and war, let us be conscious that it is because of the Christian imperative itself that we have chosen to walk in a difficult path."

The highest governing body of the Sisters of Loretto, aware that we had sisters involved in revolution in Latin America, sisters who marched from Selma to Montgomery against our racist system and those who protested the Vietnam war, stated:

"The courage of a Sister of Loretto to act on her Christian conviction deserves the support of her sisters. A common application of the Gospel to any public issue may never be reached by us, but respect for another's integrity and conscience is a value we affirm and pledge ourselves to preserve."

Globe Democrat, 1969

Sister Helen Sanders, S.L, my provincial superior, devoted a chapter entitled "Conflicting Values Surface" in her book *More Than a Renewal* (1982, Sisters of Loretto) to the Dow action. In response to the Nerinx parents who requested my dismissal from the staff, she wrote, "This we refuse to do. We hereby reassert our support of Sister Joann as a member of the Sisters of Loretto and as a faculty member at Nerinx Hall." She took this position in the face of declining enrollment and serious loss of revenue for the school for the next fifteen years. The Sisters of Loretto acted on their principles of putting human life and spiritual values before material gain, acting in a counter-capitalist manner.

I did not act alone, I was firmly rooted in a community of women, courageous ancestors, who had stood up strongly against injustice, racism, war and now the very capitalist system that supported and promoted these wrongs against human bodies. They were revolutionaries!

How to Speak to Hatred and Ignorance?

I had been teaching in the classroom, marching in demonstrations, working among the poor in Kansas City and St. Louis for five years, since my awakening to racism in Alabama. I had helped organize other non-violent actions against police brutality and the draft and now faced serious prison time.

It took an extreme form of action to get the attention of both people opposed to racism and war and those supportive of our white supremacist patriarchal church and government.

Was one effect of our action to solidify the opposition, make them more afraid and entrenched in their views? Some of the hate mail that continued to pour in seemed to indicate that:

- "Creating unrest throughout our country plays into the Communist plan to take over the country."

- "Hooray for the Dow napalm that helps more Americans come back alive"

- "We certainly cannot afford to have people like you disregarding the rights and freedoms…if we always went by what our conscience tells us, I believe this country would be in utter ruin."

- "If we condone Sister Joann's law-breaking then we open the floodgates for every anarchist in the country."

I knew I could not speak sanely to mobs or to answer all the hate mail. But this brief moment to speak to the press, to take dozens of offers to speak before college audiences and to do interviews with open-minded reporters was a rare opportunity.

So, I tried to remain human, to allow my regret for hurting people I loved and the sadness at leaving teaching be present in my face. I showed by my action of leaving the classroom at Nerinx Hall that I understood that my decision to stop teaching freed the school to function. But the hatred and misunderstanding HURT - not only hatred of me, my motives, my actions but hatred of people suffering and dying daily in our cities and in Vietnam.

I wanted to speak with the calm and clarity Thich Nhat Hanh had in responding to that heckler a year ago, to somehow reach hearts and minds filled with fear of change.

MURDERED IN THEIR BEDS

Breonna Taylor/Police Lynching of Women!

250 Murders 2015-2020

An important article in the Washington Post puts Breonna Taylor's 2020 murder into context:

> "Breonna Taylor was murdered in a no knock, nighttime home raid by Louisville, KY police on March 13, 2020. No officers have been formally charged with her murder. Her brutal killing brought into focus an often overlooked but consistent subset of people fatally shot by police - women."
>
> — Marisa Iati

Protest Advocating to Say HER Name: Breonna Taylor

Of the 247 women known to be killed in this way in the last five years, 48 were Black.

At least 89 of them were killed in their homes.

There were 1,274 Black men killed by police in the same time period.

The shooting with circumstances most similar to Breonna Taylor's murder was that of Alteria Woods, 21, who was killed March 19, 2017 in Gifford, FL. In both cases, the women were in bed and were not the subject of the police presence. No officers have been charged in her murder.

India Kager, 27, was also killed when police were "looking for someone else." In September 2015 in Virginia Beach, VA, officers threw a flash bang grenade at their parked car, and fired thirty rounds into India and her boyfriend Angelo Perry, killing both.

Their 4-month old son in the back seat was uninjured - physically. I wonder how the story of his parents death might affect the rest of his life.

The Commonwealth's attorney ruled the shooting justified.

Most of these women murdered by police were in their mid-30s or younger, but 72-year-old Geraldine Townsend was shot and killed in Bartlesville, OK on January 17, 2018, as her son Michael screamed, "That's my mother! It's a BB gun! You killed my mother."

Of the women killed since 2015, about 30% had mental health challenges, compared with 22% of the 5,362 men killed by police. The family of DeCynthia Clements, a 34 year-old woman with schizophrenia and bipolar disorder, was fatally shot in Elgin, IL. Her family says that police should have recognized that she was in the throes of a crisis and "taken steps to de-escalate the situation."

Why are police allowed to kill so many innocent people, without consequences?

Why are so many people with mental illness not receiving treatment?

Are police trained to deal with mental illness?

Domestic abuse?

Why not use conflict resolution skills rather than guns and assault weapons and grenades?

Why shoot to kill?

Why do we allow no-knock laws to exist?

Are police the ones we need to call for mental illness and domestic abuse?

WHY DO WE ALLOW THESE MURDERS TO CONTINUE?

ARE THESE MURDERS NOT A 21st CENTURY FORM OF LYNCHING?

I wouldn't know about most of these murders if not for good journalism like this article, the increase in citizens taping instances of police brutality, awareness due to #Black Lives Matter, #Say the Names, #cantwait, protests, civil suits, investigation, and the day-to-day pressure we must bring to change policies that allow police to kill with impunity.

My granddaughter sent me a quote from her Instagram discussions with other college students about police reform - "It is impossible to reform a police state. The system is not broken. It was designed to oppress and has been doing that perfectly. The police, since their inception (as slave catchers), have always upheld white supremacy as an institution. There is an uninterrupted continuum of anti-Black violence throughout the history of the American police force. ("How the U.S. got its police force," 2017 and *Stamped from the Beginning*)."

If this view seems too radical, you might feel moved to at least investigate your local police department and ask questions. Ask for a list of weapons they have, ask what their policies are on choke-holds, warnings, no-knock entry, exhausting all alternatives before shooting, learning to shoot to maim rather than kill. Are police given training in alternatives to violence, diversity, conflict resolution, meditation? Join local organizations who ask these questions, investigate, conduct training, assist with the underlying problems that cause violence. And if we think that "Defund the Police" is too radical, what ARE we doing to stop the killing by police?

When we read articles like this one on the murders of women by police, when we see a video of George Floyd's brutal murder, most of us are moved, but often feel that "it could never happen to me." Are you sure? The majority of police killings of women happened to white women! And when such brutal murders of women who are not even suspects in a crime happen without consequences for their killers, are we affected? Are we not part of this system we live in? Benefit from? Do we become 'bystanders' when allies are needed?

Remember "First they came…"

First they came for the socialists, and I did
    not speak out—
Because I was not a socialist.

> Then they came for the trade unionists, and
>> I did not speak out—
> Because I was not a trade unionist.
> Then they came for the Jews, and I did not
>> speak out—
> Because I was not a Jew.
> Then they came for me—
> and there was no one left to speak for me.
>
> — MARTIN NEIMOLLER

OR BETTER YET - THIS great film version I showed often in my high school classrooms: The Hangman (1964-Animation).

Fred Hampton/Black Panther Party

December, 1969

When I first heard the circumstances of Breonna Taylor's murder, it took me back to the murder of Fred Hampton in Chicago on December 4, 1969. His murder hit me personally because by the winter of 1969, Chicago had become another home. I had grown to love and respect the Black Panthers in my travels and speaking engagements around the country. They were particularly important to expanding my mind, my revolutionary ideas. Their analysis seemed so clear and self-evident.

Fred Hampton's young voice was powerful!

"You can kill a revolutionary, but you can't kill the revolution!"

The video can be found at: Fred Hampton: "You Can Jail A Revolutionary, But You Can't Jail A Revolution"

I was particularly impressed with the strong speeches of the Black Panther chairman of the Illinois chapter. He held rallies once a week in Chicago, urging education, health care, police observation and coalition with other revolutionary groups. He founded the Rainbow Coalition with the Lords, one of several street gangs, the Brown Berets, the Red Guard and the SDS (Students for a Democratic Society). This may have been seen by the FBI as one of his most "dangerous" actions - bringing many other groups, Black, brown and white together to fight racism, capitalism and growing fascism. Similar efforts toward unity had also been true of FBI fear of Martin Luther King when he broadened his discussion of racism to include the systematic killing of people of color in Vietnam.

Some of Fred's powerful speeches included these calls to action:

"You can jail a revolutionary, but you can't jail the revolution."

"Nothing is more important than stopping fascism, because fascism will stop us all."

"If you live til 19 or 99, if you haven't made a commitment for change, you haven't lived at all."

This last statement became his epitaph. At age 21, he was drugged by an informant and gunned down in his bed by FBI agents at 4:00am, next to his 9-month pregnant girlfriend. His friend Mark Clark, the guard at the door of the apartment, was also killed and others wounded and charged with "shooting" at federal agents. All the bullets fired - over 90 - were from the agents' guns. One shot in the ceiling came from the gun Mark Clark held when he was shot. Even the courts eventually saw this attack as murder and gave monetary awards to the young men's mothers. It was a massacre of a rising, powerful young revolutionary who struck fear into the hearts of men in power such as FBI director Hoover.

The similarities to the recent murder of Breonna Taylor in her bed by police are striking. Over fifty years later, we are still fighting the systematic slaughter of Black people. No knock laws are lethal and must be outlawed.

IN COOK COUNTY MEN'S JAIL

1969

I had no intention of getting arrested this time! I especially had no intention of getting stuck in Chicago for six weeks! I had so much to do, so many cities where I needed to speak, attend trials, organize more actions. I was minding my business in the courtroom, waiting for a hearing for the "Chicago 15," straining to see my friends Don, Tom, Linda, Margie, Bill and Ed. They had destroyed nearly 50,000 draft files on May 25, 1969, essentially wiping out the draft records of the predominantly African American South Side. I had worked with several of them on the draft file part of our action in D.C. and was happy they had a second chance to destroy files here in Chicago so effectively.

The bailiff walked in the side door, shouted "All rise." Judge Edwin Robson stalked to his dais. He seemed nervous, edgy, pulling at the sleeves of his black robe, twisting around to make sure the chair was behind him. Then he looked directly at me in the second row, shook his arm and pointed. The bailiff repeated, "All rise!" In a louder voice. I must have hesitated, glared back at the judge, done something to annoy him. All of a sudden, the bailiff was striding toward me, another bailiff came from behind me and lifted me out of my pew, marching me up to the judge's raised throne. Apparently I had not stood up quickly enough.

"Name?"

"Sister Joann Malone, S.L"

"You're a nun? You don't look like one."

"Yes, your honor, I am a member of the Sisters of Loretto.

Residence? Profession?"

"I live and teach in St. Louis, Missouri - at Nerinx Hall High School."

"What are you doing here in the courtroom today?"

"I'm here to support the defendants in the Chicago 15 hearing."

"Do you realize that you committed an act of contempt of court by not standing for me when ordered?"

"I did not intend to stay seated, your honor; but I must admit that my respect for the courts of this country is low." (I could hear my 'good angel' on my shoulder, saying "Did you have to say that Joann!")

"Perhaps ten days in jail will give you time to think about that statement!"

The judge banged the gavel, and I was dragged out the side door, passing my friends in their orange jump-suits, ready to enter the courtroom. We smiled at one another. I shrugged my shoulders, indicating that I was confused about what had just happened.

Later that afternoon, I was joined in the courthouse cell by Patricia Kennedy, a teenager from California with long, curly blond hair, jeans, t-shirt and plenty of attitude. She had apparently received a 30-day sentence for not standing up quickly enough for the same judge at the conclusion of the Chicago 15 hearing. Three times the sentence I received for an infraction usually not considered particularly important in a courtroom setting.

Pat was a total resistor, trained in non-violence techniques to completely resist arrest and cooperation with police, guards and other authority figures. So, every time we were moved - from the courthouse to Cook County Jail, from various locations in the jail, back to the courthouse - she resisted, went limp. The guards' patience with this tactic wore thin quickly. They took to shoving, grabbing, kicking and tossing her into elevators, down stairwells, having to carry her to vans. I screamed at them to be careful, that she was a minor, a kid, that they didn't have to be so rough.

When both of us ended up in the men's section of the Cook County Jail, I wondered if we would even make it out alive.

We were led, handcuffed, after processing, past row after row of cells, filled with men yelling, making lewd sexual comments, laughing at two women in their male space. The level of noise, shouting, the banging on the metal bars frightened us. Hands reached out to grab us, some white, probably most Black. I don't honestly remember, but the number of Black men in jails and prisons in the US far outweighed their numbers in the population already. The guards shoved us into a cell by ourselves, thank goodness. I felt safer there than in the hands of the guards.

I was in that cell in Cook County jail with Pat Kennedy for four days and nights, scared to our toes, unable to sleep. I was grateful to be with another woman, especially this teenager who inspired me with her commitment to non-violent resistance. We told each other our stories, nodded at the names of mutual friends in the movement. I was worried that I would miss Tom Smit's trial in Minneapolis for burning his draft card. I didn't want to be in jail right now, definitely not in this awful place. I had obligations to speak for the Chicago 15, places to go, things to do. It was a very different experience from the D.C. Women's Detention Center, where we had expected to stay until arraignment for the DC-9 action.

I'm sure that Pat had plans also, since she would participate in one of my favorite draft file actions in less than a month - the Women against Daddy Warbucks. On July 2, five women confiscated over 6,000 draft files for New York City, shredded them and dumped them off the Rockefeller Building in NY. They did not stand around to be arrested. The movement was shifting tactics, as younger, less established, reputable,well-supported activists joined actions.

We fasted, didn't eat any of the food again, so it kept us safer in our cells. I suppose they brought us water, but I don't remember a shower or getting outdoors for the four days and nights we were there. Just as well, if it meant walking that phalanx of shouters and bar-bangers again.

Conspiracy 8 group, 1968

It seemed that Judge Robson had over-reacted in sentencing us to the men's jail. As Pat and I talked and shared our experiences in the courtroom, we realized that he must have been reacting to the uproar around the Conspiracy 8 hearings. The eight had been charged with conspiracy to create riots in the Democratic Convention in July 1968. They were indicted in March and had a hearing in the same federal building where the Chicago 15 hearing took place that June day. The lines to gain admittance to see Bobby Seale, Abbie Hoffman, Jerry Rubin, Rennie Davis and the rest went around the entire block. We were fortunate to gain access to the building. The tension among the judges and bailiffs must have been high in anticipation of disturbance to their courtrooms. (For a modern version of their trial see "The Chicago Seven" on Netflix.)

I had read everything I could find on the Black Panther Party after befriending Leon Clark and Robert Coen of the Black Liberators. I would have loved to meet Bobby Seale, the co-founder of the Black Panther Party. I wondered if he was housed here in the same jail. But Pat pointed out that his case was federal, so he was probably in a different prison. I knew that wherever he was at that moment, his conditions would be much worse than mine. As a Black man in prison, he might never be released. His treatment - eventually chained to his chair in the courtroom, gagged and bound at his own trial - was outrageous. He did not ask to be charged with conspiracy nor contempt (a charge that would gain him a four-year sentence in a few months). But we both shared contempt for this unjust system.

His history of speaking out against the systematic oppression and killing of Black people, his role of forming an armed group to oppose police brutality was his real "crime." In the "Ten Point Platform" he and Huey Newton published, they made clear their demands:

"- We Want An Immediate End To Police Brutality And Murder Of Black People.

- We Want Freedom For All Black Men held In federal, state, county and city prisons and jails.

- We Want All Black People when brought to trial to be tried in court by a jury of their Peer Group or People From Their Black Communities, as defined by the Constitution of the United States (Cannon 1970,15-16)."

These demands are so similar to today's Black Lives Matter movement!

Our white skin, middle-class privilege showed itself once again. On the fifth day, Pat and I were bailed out of Cook County jail by the ACLU. Our friends in the Chicago 15 had contacted lawyers. They thought our case would be a good one to set a precedent for courtroom rights. Ironic that I wanted to be free in order to commit more crimes - plan more anti-war, antiracist, anti-system actions!

So, the lawyers convinced us to come out on bail while they tried the case. It turned into a six-week semi-imprisonment in Chicago for me! A longer sentence really, with restrictions that I couldn't leave the city, couldn't speak publicly, cause trouble, get arrested for anything else. I stayed with friends from the Chicago 15, growing to love the city; but I didn't follow the judge's rules.

A complete Catch-22, since I could be locked up indefinitely if I didn't appear in person for my weekly parole report in St. Louis for the Dow Chemical Action! I still faced 35 years on those charges. So, I had to take a chance. The Chicago judge wouldn't find out that I hitch-hiked once a week to report in St. Louis, a pattern that gave me dozens of great experiences talking to truck drivers about war, racism and the effects on their lives. If they got "fresh" with me, I either asked them about their wives and children or told them that I was a nun. That usually stopped any amorous views toward this long-haired, jean-wearing hitch-hiker nun.

One of my most memorable hitches happened in Detroit during this period. I had a speaking engagement to preach at a church there, so I took a chance on leaving Chicago for that purpose, but had to get back for a court hearing. My friend Dennis of the DC-9, a priest from a poor Black neighborhood in Detroit, dropped me near the ramp to the highway just before a sudden rainstorm broke. I knew it would be difficult to get a ride in the rain, but held up my sign in one hand and umbrella in the other.

A car pulled up that appeared to be already full of people. The mother in the front seat gestured to me to get in the back seat with the kids. I quickly folded the umbrella, tossed it on the floor and squeezed in the back with three kids, each holding a bag of groceries!

The kindness of this African American family blew me away! To stop, with groceries and a full car, to pick up a strange, wet white woman and drive out of their way to drop me at a safe spot with shelter was an act of compassion that stays with me to this day.

THE PRISON PROJECT

2020

Ta-Nahesi Coates in a recent interview said, "I feel like the need to have an opinion on everything at every moment corrupts thinking." So he quit Twitter in 2017 and his job at Atlantic in 2018. I saw him testifying at a Congressional hearing on reparations for slavery, jostling in the hallway with dozens of others trying to find space in the room. I've been a fan of his compelling voice since I read *Between the World and Me* and *The Water Dancer*. His courageous writing reveals both his love for American ideals while clearly seeing that the US does not live up to them for the African American people. He celebrates Kamala Harris' victory but knows that it doesn't equal restoring all the damage done by the last administration. He said "There's a beauty in seeing certain things, even if those things make you sometimes sad, or despairing or they hurt you. But I would rather know than not."

He lives with his eyes open because he must. There is danger in believing the dream without looking at today's reality. Danger for himself, for the son he is educating in *Between the World and Me*. "The beauty of Black people is hard-earned and hard to see. It's tough. It comes with people's attitudes and people's thoughts and their dysfunctions...but when you see it, it's the most beautiful thing in the world. I would never want to be anywhere else. I would never give this up (Washington Post, 2020)."

I get it. I see the beauty in African American lives and culture and celebrate it without ever wanting to ignore the long road we must still travel to true equality. I also relate to the depth of his despair about the slowness of change in this country's systemic racism and the love and beauty that keeps us going. I was strongly tempted to leave the country when I faced thirty-five years in federal prison at my sentencing in the spring of 1970, two days after students were killed by national guardsmen at Kent State. Would Cuba take a federal felon ex-nun with a baby? I stayed, knowing I could never completely cut myself off from this country and its people. We were too inter-connected, injustices, faults, set-backs and all. The beauty, the ideals, the love kept me grounded where I had been planted, where I must keep growing and speaking out.

1970

The Prison Project

Prisons steal babies/Ericka Huggins

The New Haven trial of Black Panther Ericka Huggins May 1969.

Within the next year, I had survived a highly publicized, brutal trial, was convicted of four of the five federal felonies, sentenced to four years in Alderson Women's Federal Prison, formally left Loretto, and became a mother, despite the FBI searching for me constantly.

Just after the Kent State and Jackson State murders of students protesting the war, we faced our sentencing in D.C. Agents of the US government were shooting students protesting non-violently - white (Kent State) and Black (Jackson State). It was the most difficult time ever to walk into the courtroom, knowing not only that I faced years of imprisonment, but that the baby I carried secretly might be taken from me by the judge, the state.

I was particularly aware of Ericka Huggins, the leader of the Black Panther Party in New Haven, Connecticut, who was arrested in May 1969 on conspiracy charges with Bobby Seale. Her husband John Huggins had been murdered by the same COINTELPRO program of the FBI that would slaughter Fred Hampton that same year (Blackstock, 1975). At the time of his murder, their daughter was only three weeks old and just five months old when Ericka was arrested and imprisoned for two years. If the government could rip her child from her and constantly threaten to remove her baby from relatives and place her in the "care" of the state, the same could happen to me. In a sense, I felt we were both political prisoners, but as a Black woman, as usual, her conditions were much more dangerous.

I knew that if the doctors examined me in jail after our sentencing, they would tell the judge and the world I was pregnant. All hell would break loose. Almost no one knew, so fear that the judge and FBI would find out terrified me. I was convinced that I would go to prison immediately at sentencing. My child would be born in prison and be taken from me, never to be seen again. I almost fled to Cuba rather than enter that courthouse, but Ericka's courage bolstered mine.

2020

Today, I wonder about Ericka and see from her website that she and I have arrived at similar paths in our elder years. We are now both teachers, writers, speakers on peace and justice. We are both daily meditators (she taught herself in solitary confinement in prison). We both see the need for a spiritual aspect to ending racism and violence today. We both reflect on the lessons of movement history:

"I still feel if we could form coalitions today with like organizations, especially women, that we would be a force to contend with. That is why we did it because we were all being stalked, infiltrated, jailed, killed, and so we formed coalitions to have strength in numbers and to support one another. We saw the beauty and the power of it (*Washington Post*, 2020)."

I think she and I would agree on the need for all people in our country to wake up to the harm racism is doing to us all and has been for over 400 years. We cannot escape the harm because of our lighter skin when our very beings are connected to all who are oppressed, stereotyped, blamed for the ills of our society. Whenever one group of people is oppressed, ALL are oppressed.

"We can together change the world. We are all threaded together like a huge tapestry of humanity. And we forget that we are interconnected."

— Ericka Huggins, "The Role of Spiritual Practice in Social Justice Work," (Bioneers, 2016)

La Lucha Continua!

The Prison Project (IPS) - 1971

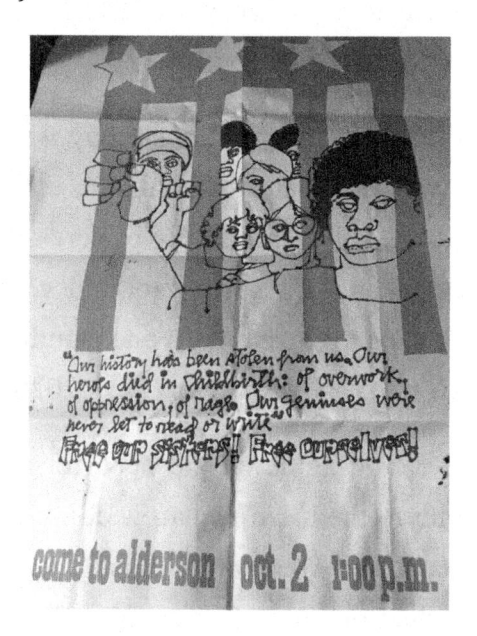

Poster (from my attic) for a demonstration at Alderson Women's Federal Prison- where my DC-9 companion Catherine Melville was imprisoned and where I was sentenced for four years. From centerfold of OFF OUR BACKS, a women's newspaper. I edited this special edition on Women in Prison in 1971.

My son's father convinced me to move back from California to the East coast with him, then left me on a farm in Virginia with a nine-month old son. I moved into D.C., joined Earth Onion Women's Improvisational Theater Group and the Prison Project at the Institute for Policy Studies. Both groups saved our lives and my sanity. The theater group gave me creative work, a voice to express feelings and stories bursting to be revealed. The women of Earth Onion became life-long friends, intimate political/social allies, commune companions and alternate mothers for my son. I would have the four-year sentence hanging over my head for the first three years of my son's life, until it was resolved on appeal that reduced my four felonies to a misdemeanor. So friendship with women and organizing for women in prison became a focus for survival and purpose.

I WAS PRIVILEGED to work at the Institute for Political Studies on an intense study of the conditions of US prisons. Arthur Waskow, a Fellow there, gave me both a job and a home with his wife Irene and his two children. We published statistics on the number of African American women and men incarcerated and analysis of prisons as an extension of slavery. Even in the '70s the numbers of Black people in prison far outweighed their numbers in the US population, and the percentages grow every year. According to the Justice Department, between 1974 and 2001, the prevalence of imprisonment increased by nearly 3.8 million. Prisons have become a multi-billion dollar industry, largely controlled by corporations like CCA. Free slave labor again! For corporations! Devastation to Black families.

One of our projects involved organizing a national conference in Chicago. I worked on that project with a powerful, brilliant African American man from L.A, David Soloman, who became a good friend.

Our local D.C. women's newspaper, *Off Our Backs*, allowed me to edit a special edition of the paper in September 1971 on Women in Prison. I interviewed women incarcerated in Alderson, WV for this project, including one of the famous Puerto Rican women who had disrupted Congress in 1954 demanding independence for their country. I also interviewed the warden, conscious that she would totally control my life at any moment I violated the conditions of my parole pending appeal of our conviction.

2020

I highly recommend watching the award-winning documentary *13th* by African American director Ava DuVernay. The testimony of Black prisoners, scholars, and activists details the history of US prisons and present conditions with far better detail and insight than I can offer.

Another classic, Angela Davis's *Are Prisons Obsolete?* questions how we have come to consider having the US (with 4% of the world's population) housing one-quarter of the prisoners in the world! She maintains that our present system grew from slavery, slave codes, and chain gangs into a "for-profit" prison industrial complex. No wonder that people of color are over 65% of the US prison population! No wonder "three-strike," indeterminate sentences, and harsh drug possession laws keep the massive number of prisons filled to capacity, making millions from misery - mental illness, poverty, domestic violence, addiction. Davis's arguments for the abolition of prisons is logical, practical, and visionary.

Angela Davis (from a poster)

Reaction to Attica at IPS

1971

"I will survive!" "I can do this." I am sitting on a folding chair, in a huge circle of intellectuals, activists, brilliant writers, and speakers at the Institute for Policy Studies in the fall of 1971. I look around the circle at our IPS leaders Marcus Raskin and Dick Barnet, at Bob Moses and Ivanhoe Donaldson, African American SNCC leaders and organizers, Betty Garman of SNCC, Charlotte Bunch Weeks and Rita Mae Brown, speaking for women's and gay liberation rights, my friend David, other new associates like myself.

On September 9, 1971, two weeks after the killing of George Jackson, 1,281 of the New York Attica Prison's approximately 2,200 inmates rioted and took control of the prison, taking 42 staff members hostage. The photos of the Black bodies stripped naked, beaten, chained together, brought back images of slave ships, chain gangs, centuries of abuse and killing.

IPS staff gathered to formulate a press release and discuss actions we could sponsor. The rhetoric flew around the room. Ivanhoe called for a Black Caucus to be formed immediately, stating that he had given up on this "white man's system" entirely. Charlotte mentioned the Prison Project that David and I had just begun, urging us to draft a strong statement that the women's movement could endorse.

My son, a toddler, whom I often brought to these large gatherings, walked around the inside of the circle, studying adult faces. He looked up, startled by an angry remark, shied away from the grabby females, and settled on one of Bob Moses' legs. I was happy that he was becoming a good judge of character since I might be leaving him for four years in a cell.

Bob had proved his courage in the SNCC voter registration campaign in Mississippi in 1961, in Freedom Summer in '64, and did training of SNCC field organizers from his IPS office. He had cut off relationships with white civil rights activists in '66 but was here trying yet again to form coalitions across different ideologies and interest groups.

He finally spoke up, the bridge voice, gentle, not wanting to frighten the small blond head leaning on his thigh:

"Attica is horrible. Truly horrible. But we have to stand up with these brave men who are risking their lives to speak out…We have to dig into ourselves and the community to wage psychological warfare…We combat our own fears about beatings, shootings, and possible mob violence. We create a small striking force capable of nonviolent action. We are never alone."

He lifted my son up into the air, provoking giggles in him and calming the whole room.

Motherhood had changed me. Would I always view ideas and actions now from a mother's eyes? I wondered what it was like for the mothers of those men in Attica, to see their sons bound and naked on the television news.

D.C. FIGHT BACK
TERRENCE JOHNSON

Changing/Organizing

I was excited by the newness of working at the Institute for Policy Studies, the intellectual stimulation I craved, the rainbow hues of the people, the voices for Black Liberation, Women's Liberation, Gay Liberation, freedom and independence for Palestine and South Africa.

I was bombarded with new language and theories, yet suffering and still healing personally from the separation from my son's father.

I listened to the voices of many artists and activist intellectuals, who had put jobs, physical safety, and lives on the line. I yearned for a more overarching worldview that would replace my "Catholic left" upbringing. I had thoroughly rejected any pretense of connection with the church by this time, although I maintained relationships with friends in the DC-9 and other actions.

Elements of the Black Panther and MaoTseTung philosophy, SNCC and Malcolm X's language, feminist and gay poetry jumbled in my head. They spoke of a vision of the future in which Black people and women had full equality, full freedom to live, learn, create and contribute to society. Brave leaders continued to emerge to resist oppression, continued to speak out, stand up for justice.

I joined a study group that would lead to ten years of intense study of socialism, a new level of commitment to total social change, and a vision of a life of equality. I saw yet another version of the beloved community Martin Luther King described emerging.

I relished the debates in the study groups.

I kept asking questions.

I remember many group discussions like this:

"I have a question about what we read from Stalin on the 'National Question.'

"Do you think that these Russian revolutionaries wanted a separate state for Black people for their liberation or to 'get them out' of Russia?"

Why don't we have more Black people in these study groups? Here in Chocolate City?" I asked.

"I'd like to know what Black people here think of all this talk of a separate Black nation. Who are we - a bunch of white radicals - to decide what Black people need?"

I could tell that my questions landed in the room like a bomb. Everyone turned to Phil, our only African American member, for an answer. It put him in an awkward and unfair position as spokesperson for all the missing Black brothers and sisters. A common form of pressure and misunderstanding I saw all the time in predominantly white groups, even with good-hearted people who wanted change. And here, I'd been the one to do it to him!

But Phil was used to it, used to be the token Black man in his wife's white world. So, he spelled it out to us - "Listen. Look at what happens to us in predominantly white groups. Our voices get drowned, pushed to the side, not heard. We're in a period now of needing Black Power groups that focus on Black history and Black liberation. We need to focus on the killings in Black communities that never get reported in the news, on police brutality. Most of you don't feel it every day, even in a majority Black city. You can escape, smoke your dope, forget this revolutionary talk for a while. But I'm always Black, everywhere I go, in every group. I have to fight as if my life depends on it because it does!"

He was right. I had unwittingly put him on the spot without intending to do so. It wasn't his responsibility to speak for all African Americans. We had a responsibility to find out for ourselves what had happened historically and what was going on now. I still had a long way to go in waking up to the subtle forms of racism even within the movement. I looked at Phil's toddler son, sucking a bottle in his lap, staring at his dad who was speaking so passionately.

I had been in a reverse position, the only white woman in an all-Black meeting at a conference on prisons, a fly on the wall, tolerated because of my prison sentence. I had heard the arguments for separate Black revolutionary groups, the grief at the loss of leaders like Fred Hampton. I understood that the Panthers and other groups wanted the independence to demand whatever was needed at the time that fostered the rights of Black people. They weren't advocating for permanent separation or the "back to Africa" notions of Marcus Garvey. Just a period of time and space to decide on their own what to do. I respected the decision, the life/death reality of it. I saw friends I had known for years gently turn their backs on white groups. It wasn't personal, but it was necessary for now. It still hurt to lose friends, even temporarily.

I longed for communities with respect and equality for both Black people and women. So, our group began to build community by starting campaigns for renters, organizing unions in factories, hospitals, and schools, supporting people of color as leaders.

On one job at the Marriott food plant's sanitation department, I was the first white woman ever hired. I enjoyed practicing my minimal French with Haitian co-workers and learning Spanish from the Dominican workers, as we cleaned toilets and picked up trash. In another temporary job in the same plant, I substituted for a woman on a bakery line whose work felt impossible - pulling off buns that were sticking to the pans on a long assembly line, alone, with two huge ovens on both sides of me roaring and sending out 400-degree heat. I screamed for help every day I worked on that assembly line, but no one could hear me. The administration decided to hide me in the print shop rather than the visible bakery and sanitation departments, but I found ways of making friends and organizing a union drive.

I learned a great deal on this job - that many of our socialist discussions romanticized the working class and the lives of African Americans. The day-to-day struggle to work this hard, to stay healthy enough to keep making a paycheck, to tolerate the abuse, speed-up, unjust transfers, and firings was about all that some people could do. Many were not willing to stick their necks out and get fired for conversing about unions. Their children needed food and clothing. A job was a matter of survival. Marriott was famous for racist and sexist practices and would do almost anything to keep unions out of their shops. There were even rumors of untimely deaths after immigration raids.

D.C. UNITE TO FIGHT BACK 1972-82

The D.C. Unite to Fight Back group I helped form lasted for several years and probably did some of our most dramatic and effective work.

The goals of the local and national Fight Back were to:

Fight for jobs or income for everyone.

Fight discrimination against minorities and women.

Fight against police repression.

Fight against deportations and for the rights of foreign-born workers.

Support workers' struggles to make the trade unions a working tool of the people, not the bosses

Support the struggles of Third-World peoples against imperialism and to oppose the imperialist war preparations by the two superpowers, the US, and the USSR.

One of the projects developed from an attempted eviction in an apartment building in the Adams-Morgan neighborhood of D.C.. This was a mixed neighborhood of poorer apartments and huge private homes. The area was predominantly African American, with some African and Latino families and a minority of whites, younger ones in apartments/older in private homes. Most of us lived in shared apartments or experimental communes. I lived with members of my theater group for years.

All of us renters had similar problems as the new immigrants from Mexico and El Salvador and African American workers - paying the rent! Facing illegal evictions. Landlords who wouldn't repair the roof, take care of plumbing.

The Fight Back waged a campaign against the eviction of several groups of African American and immigrant workers in the neighborhood where we also lived. By holding demonstrations, organizing rent refusal, pooling resources to block evictions, we formed a solid group. Eventually we won stronger tenant laws, saved families' homes, won hearts and minds to our wider demands for jobs and equality for people of color and women.

In addition to writing local flyers, we described our victories in the national newspaper we had formed, The Call, which helped us and our new Fight Back organizers see that their problems were not unique, that people of color, women, workers, immigrants all over the country were also fighting back against unjust laws, bosses, and landlords.

"El Pueblo Unido Jamás será Vencido!" Still rings in my ears from those demonstrations, along with the hugs and smiles of children sensing the power in resisting together. "The people united will never be defeated!"

The Terrence Johnson Campaign 1978

Terrence Johnson

One of the benefits of my job at Marriott was the relationship with Jeff, an African American man who had worked in the freezer there for years. We hung out after work, discussing conditions in the plant, how to form a union. We became good friends.

Jeff and I were watching the news on the night of June 26, 1978, when I saw a photo of a young Black teenager, his arrest photo, flash on the screen. The announcer said that he had just shot two white policemen in the Hyattsville station, only two miles from our apartment. "Oh, my God, I shouted, "they're going to kill that kid! What can we do?" I grabbed the phone, called my friend Randy in the Fight Back group, and told him the story. Within minutes, several members of the D.C. Unite to Fight Back had spread the word and found a lawyer who promised to go directly to the Hyattsville holding facility. Jeff and I grabbed poster paper and markers, jumped in the car, and sped to Hyattsville, determined to rouse the press, to keep their eyes on this young man. We prayed that we wouldn't be too late, that angry cops would not end his life in retaliation, as had happened to so many other young Black men.

15-year-old Terry and his brother Melvin, then 18, were stopped by officers Claggett and Swart who thought their father's car matched the description of a car near the robbery of some washing machines. Melvin had woken Terry from sleep to take a ride with him. Terry was a good student, had never been involved in any criminal activity, and this was his first encounter with police. Both boys were arrested, cuffed, and beaten. Terry had no experience, answered too slowly, and was taken into a small room alone by Officer Claggett who said, "I'm gonna break your neck." Against the rules, Claggett kept his gun on his hip as he held Terry by the neck. In the struggle, Terry grabbed the gun handle, fired, and kept wild-firing the gun as he ran out of the small room, hitting

Officer Swart also. His brother, still cuffed to a cell in the larger room, along with two white teenagers waiting for their parents, could have been shot also.

Miraculously Terry survived that night, a long, difficult trial, a 25-year sentence and 15 years in prison. The Prince George's County police had a decades-long history of brutality, false arrests, beatings of African Americans. Claggett had been involved in the beating of Thomas Peet the year before; after filing a complaint, Thomas was found drowned to death. We knew that getting good legal representation and keeping the truth before the eyes of the community was necessary to Terry's continued survival.

Members of the Fight Back demonstrated, raised money for his defense, support for the trial, and exposed the history of police abuse and murders of other Black men. I remember well driving around D.C. and Prince George's County, picking up teenagers who wanted to attend the trial, march in front of the courthouse in Upper Marlboro. We also visited his family over many years, testified before parole hearings, wrote to him, visited him. Pressure from the Prince George's County police union kept delaying the parole of a man who completed high school, college, and pre-law courses in prison. Finally, in 1995, he was released with a full scholarship to Howard University's law school.

By the '90s I was telling his story to young Black teenagers in the D.C. schools.

The end of Terrence Johnson's story is a sad, disappointing one. After his release from prison, he went to law school, worked for his lawyer/mentor, had a girlfriend. But, desperate for money, he participated in a robbery two years later, with another brother, and shot himself to death rather than go back to jail.

2020

This business of remaining committed to relationships and to the struggle for racial equality, no matter what, is difficult, often full of personal suffering. It is the very suffering, the constancy of the oppression that keeps me waking up today. The temptation is always there to walk away. My white privilege tells me it's possible for me to do that, to walk away. I suppose I tried to escape all the intensity by drinking in those days when relationships soured, when union drives failed, when the daily grind of poverty and racial attacks seemed so overwhelming.

But I know now that my life depends now on continuing to stay awake, to awaken more and more, to face the reality of what racism does to us all. Racism is a disease, similar to this Covid pandemic killing people all over the world, similar to my alcoholism. It demands alertness, awareness, mindfulness to be able to change racist policies, attitudes, and power.

If I fall asleep, close my eyes and ears to cries for justice, something in my soul begins to die.

LIVING IN A BLACK FAMILY

Writing this book about racism has, I hoped, helped me be more aware of my own prejudices and perked up my ears to subtly racist views I hear from other white folks. In *How to Be an Antiracist*, Ibram Kendi points out that anyone at any time can take racist or antiracist actions, including Black people, including Black leaders like W.E.B DuBois. It's our actions, our work to change policy that counts more than attitude.

I've had two conversations recently that surprised me about how we good-intentioned white people can support racist views, often without being aware. We all need constant education and reminders of this antiracist perspective, and I still need to "be woken up."

A friend who lives in a predominately white world shared a photo of a sign that said, "All Lives Matter." She felt it made a broader statement than "Black Lives Matter," I suppose. I told her that "No, I wouldn't be interested in it," and why. I explained that in this climate of the Black Lives Matter movement, it could be interpreted as a response that said, "You're wrong. I know more than you do." The reality is that Black people are being targeted daily, killed with impunity by police. White people need to stand up and say loudly, clearly –

"BLACK LIVES MATTER!!! STOP the KILLING!!!"

General statements such as "All lives matter," while obvious and true, are insensitive and tend to dismiss the cries of African Americans to everyone to see the reality of racism and DO something!

Another well-meaning white friend spoke of a project we were working on together as having two panels of people "in the same social circles." Code for "BLACK," I realized. I had the opposite reaction to the meeting we had where the representation of People of Color had increased. I was thrilled that we had made advances over the predominantly white planning committee of last year's event. We don't change the composition of any group without conscious effort, without noticing racial imbalance, without inviting African American and Latino friends to join, to lead, to be heard.

So often, white people who have not had intimate, long friendships with African Americans, who might not have participated in groups with strong Black leadership, miss subtle acts and words of exclusion.

Becoming Part of a Black Family

1978

Three African American men who had worked in the freezer at Marriott's Fairfield Farms Kitchens for many years seemed to be our best possibilities to form a new union organizing campaign. Wilson, King, and Jeff drove forklifts in and out of sub-zero freezers all day. They were covered in thick, padded jackets, pants and hoods, so I wouldn't have recognized them on the street. Their mustaches and small beards were tipped with frozen icicles. I began to notice them while I worked in sanitation, whipping out of the freezer with pallets-full of products for the bakery or kitchen. They thought it was funny to see a white woman in a red hard hat pushing a huge trash container, nudging one another, laughing at me. I waved back, smiling.

By the time I had moved to the print shop, I had to manufacture excuses to walk to the freezer or bakery and make contact with friends. I grabbed every opportunity possible to deliver printed forms or mail to other parts of the huge plant.

Before long, I was able to arrange meetings outside the plant, and found myself drinking a beer after work with Jeff and Wilson on the street corner. It was a rough part of town, so I guess I had a self-image of being some badass, tough-gal union organizer or something. Arrogant looking back on it now.

I learned more about their lives, families and concerns. Wilson had a wife and two small children but loved PCP; he eventually ruined his liver with drinking and drugs. King was married too, happily so, but Jeff was single. He made me laugh, invited me to tag along to the Captain's Table, a local bar, after work on the back of his motorcycle. I was motivated to learn more about the previous union drive; he was looking for a more personal connection.

One day, Jeff stopped me in the hallway, after coming to look for me. He passed me a photo of a young boy - a four-year-old exact replica of the man in front of me, with the same distinct Asian slant in his eyes. Jeff's nickname was "The Yang." He was in shock and needed to share the news with a friend. Apparently a distant cousin with whom he had gotten drunk at a wedding had given birth to his child without telling him. Now, broken up with her boyfriend, she needed help. He told me his family adored children, that he needed to step up and help her out. I agreed with him, told him that he wouldn't have a chance denying he was the father. Any judge looking at that photo would order child support.

Eventually Jeff and I became a couple, rotating time between his apartment in the Marbury Plaza in SE D.C. and mine in Mt. Rainier. His cousin, Vonnie lived in the Marbury Plaza apartments too, with a roommate, Rock whose main income came from dealing drugs. I had stopped any casual drug use in order to become a founding member of a political group several years earlier (since infiltrators were notorious for getting us in trouble on minor drug charges, a distraction from the serious work of overthrowing the state!). But Jeff's friends were heavy drinkers too, so I joined in on that legal activity. I reveled in the dancing, partying and relaxing. I hadn't had this much fun since my women's theater days. The revolution could get a bit serious and grim sometimes.

After a year or so, Jeff made the huge decision to let go of his apartment and move into a two bedroom with me in Mt. Rainier, MD. It was an act of trust in me for someone who highly valued his independence. By then the mother of his son had moved closer to D.C. and he visited Teddy, brought him to family gatherings, and sent her regular child support.

We lived together for five years, splitting costs for the apartment, utilities and food, my son living with us full-time. His father had become more present in his life by this time, inviting him to spend the night a couple of times a week. So he didn't need Jeff to be a father figure.

One of the greatest long-term values of this time with Jeff was becoming the minority, often the only white person in an all-Black family and circle of friends. I loved his mother and grandmother, both of whom accepted me completely. After a few moments of my awkwardness, they embraced me, led me to the table to plate up, handed me a beer and continued sharing the latest family news. Pictures of the surprise grandson were passed around and pledges made to make sure Teddy was present for Christmas - my son too!

Jeff's aunt's attitude was cooler toward me, protective of her nephew, wondering what I wanted from him. As my drinking habit increased, I can see now that she thought I wasn't worthy of Jeff. She and her husband had high level jobs in the Maryland government and looked down on me as unemployed. They were educated, middle-class, comfortable. I was working full-time by then on the Terrence Johnson campaign for the D.C. Unite to Fight Back, living on savings and unemployment. Aunt Jackie demonstrated her displeasure in me by putting me at the kids' table at Thanksgiving, while Jeff was asked to sit at the main table with his brother and his gorgeous new African American girlfriend. It was another time in my life I felt outclassed. I also experienced the resentment some Black women felt against white women for "stealing" an eligible Black man. I was in the position that Black people have every day, in every situation in a white-dominated, white-controlled world. Where white is seen as the norm and everyone, every nuance of life is judged in comparison to the white norm. It was good for me to live the reverse of this pattern. It gave me a tiny insight into what being Black in a white world must be like.

Jeff's younger friends were more accepting of me, as we partied together, discussed racism, sexism, families, jobs. His cousin, Vonnie, and I were both actively involved in demonstrations, organizing and studying Black history, discussing various political views late into the night. I still miss him, would love to know what he's doing today in the Black Lives Matter movement.

I remember one time the three of us rushing to dress up for a fancy Christmas dinner at the Hay Adams Hotel for my television job. Walking out the door we realized that both Jeff and my son were wearing tennis shoes. We had to make a quick stop at Payless in the mall nearby to attempt to play Cinderella for a night. We laughed all the way downtown in the car.

We adapted to one another's cultural differences. Jeff, a city guy, came with me frequently to the Shenandoah Mountains, climbing Old Rag, sleeping on old mattresses on the living room floor with ten theater friends. I learned the Electric Slide and the art of turning any gathering of three people into a party.

Much was similar in our working class backgrounds. I experienced the same work ethic in Jeff's family I was taught, showing up on Monday no matter how much we partied on the weekend. Loyalty to family, keeping secrets and protecting one another in trouble, resilience, and love, always love. Often I envisioned a beautiful second child with him, perhaps with those slanted eyes, his smooth skin, his smile.

I learned a great deal in the experience of living in a Black family. Even with support from friends, we both felt judgement and discrimination for our inter-racial relationship.

MY SON JOINED a local Cub Scout group and went to meetings in a home near our apartment complex. The den mother wanted to recruit me to help, so she invited our family to join hers in a cookout.

Then came the nervous call. "Ahh…hi, Joann…about the cookout…I didn't realize that Jeff was….ahh…"

"Black?" I said.

"Yes," she answered with some relief at not having to mouth the word.

"So, you're trying to say that we're no longer invited to your home?"

"It would be a problem for some of my neighbors… not us, you understand."

"Well, that means it's a problem for us too. I don't really want my son to be involved with a group that promotes racism. He doesn't either."

It was one small moment of having to speak the truth, to stand up for who we were, to demonstrate finding a way to live together and celebrate our multicultural world. Not cave in to the narrow prejudices and stereotypes of our white neighbors. But also not to descend to nastiness and sarcasm.

I know my response to the cub scout den mother probably had an edge of disappointment and anger. I had not yet developed the ability to speak with grace, compassion and generosity in situations like this.

I MISSED Jeff's mother and grandmother for years after our alcoholism led us to an ugly break-up. The ending was so definite and violent, steeped in our mutual disease of alcoholism, that it was impossible for me to stay connected to any members of his family. I felt the separation as a huge loss, especially since they filled a deep need in me for family. I had left my birth family for good at age 17, and lived too far away to see them more than every few years. Jeff's family had become mine, but now, I had to sever the ties to survive.

2020

I found out that he passed several years ago. His brother got word to me, but never responded to my emails afterwards. I would love to connect to him, to Jeff's cousin, Vonnie, who was my good friend forty years ago. My Google search found Jeff's obituary from 2010, with a comment by Vonnie, but so far I have not been able to find my old friend.

My relationship with Jeff had many good years, full of fun, real love, family, deep lessons, but the ending was tragic. Our alcoholism led us to hurt one another and remain separated for the rest of his life.

The suffering eventually helped me find a new spiritual path.

Looking back on it, I know that living with Jeff wasn't a mere political statement. We loved one another as best we could, given who we were at the time, given our mutual suffering and limitations. We lived together, were a unit, a family, part of his large, tight family, part of the Fight Back family.

In addition to working hard, trying to change society, we had fun, loyalty, laughter. We laughed every day. He was good at turning almost any situation into humor, sometimes aggravating my serious revolutionary determination.

RECOVERY

The speeches at the Democratic Convention this summer shook me back to 1984, to the crisis ending my relationship with Jeff, right before flying to San Francisco to manage the Democratic Convention news coverage for five television stations.

Just out of the hospital from my last encounter with my lover, still swollen and bruised, I painted on a professional face, ignored the comments and threw myself into a very demanding job with the Washington Post television division. We covered the Democratic convention in San Francisco and the Republican in Dallas. Among duties ordering satellite service, coordinating reporters, cameramen and engineers' needs, I also threw parties for the networks. The television job was something I had fallen into as a temporary secretary to pay bills. Now it enabled me to drown my sorrows at the failed relationship and disappointing electoral politics scene.

I was emotionally drained, physically addicted to alcohol, a work-a-holic in charge for years of the company happy hours and parties. I didn't realize that the drinking was such a problem until I found myself alone, without Jeff and his friends to blame for the abundance of liquor in my life. I thought he was the problem, but I was still drinking around the clock. I tried every day to stop, but I needed it, every day, every hour.

I had become a very different woman from the nun and courageous member of the DC-9. Stuck in a television job that had no activist purpose for social change, avoiding old friends who might see the changes in my life, I blamed everyone and everything outside myself for my anger and despair.

My recovery story is another book in itself. But as it relates to this theme of waking up to racism, the process gave me a host of African American friends who became supporters for building a new way of life and finding a new spiritual path. For me, this involved reaching a depth of despair and hopelessness that forced me to beg for help, to realize I needed other people. Today daily recovery meetings and deep relationships with people of all classes, genders, ethnicities and cultures give me constant contact with real suffering and fellowship.

1985

My first meeting was in the spring of 1985 at the "180 Club" in Hyattsville, less than a block from the building where Terrence Johnson's life changed forever. The majority of people at the club were Black, but there were also many Latinos, whites, young, old, some professionally dressed and some coming from construction jobs. After several meetings, I experienced what still feels like a miracle (without hospitals or treatment) - 24 hours without a drink. Something I had not experienced for at least seven years, trying as hard as possible to stop. Over these last thirty-five years of sobriety, I have been helped by people of many ethnic groups, ages, religious views, classes and political persuasions. Alcoholism is a deadly disease that honors no social boundary, no politics, education or ideology.

What binds us is the single purpose of staying sober and helping other alcoholics to achieve sobriety, one day at a time. I could never have reached a day of sobriety on my own, let alone years. Today my life depends on daily contact with other alcoholics, working the twelve steps of recovery and avoiding only one drink - that first one. The hardest part for me, a confirmed atheist for the last ten years or so of my drinking, was accepting a spiritual path as the solution for my problems. I had deeply rejected religion, feeling that humans had created poverty, wars, racism, sexism and it was up to us to change.

One friend, Marvin, a handsome, older Black man who once held a job at the White House, comforted me in my struggles with trying to find a Higher Power. He had also been raised in a religious tradition, Southern Baptist, and turned away from it years ago. We often discussed feeling real power and energy in meetings, wanting a new spiritual path, but resisting anything to do with religion. He suggested that I try taking walks outdoors, enjoy the sun, the rain, the trees and mountains. "I just know that whatever power keeps the earth moving, the grass growing, the sun coming up is good," he said. We shared an interest in Native American spirituality, especially in the view of earth, nature, animals, the Great Spirit that connects us to others. I followed his advice, relaxed, watched my life and his life keep changing and expanding. He still frequently reminds me that the program of recovery is not religious, that folks are free to find whatever spirit helps them stay sober.

Today, my friends in recovery keep me grounded in the reality of real daily suffering and constant transformation of suffering into doing the next right thing. My own life and their lives are testimony to the reality that anything, anyone can change.

No matter what it takes, I intend to stay sober, one day at a time. No matter what it takes, I intend to become an antiracist, to do my part to build a "beloved community." Change is possible. I see it happening every day.

Inspiration in Recovery Meetings

2020

Since early March, 2020, all my recovery meetings have gone to zoom. The beauty of this medium is that I can find meetings all over the world, anytime of day or night. There's no excuse for not staying in touch with my fellow alcoholics, being constantly inspired by them, knowing that we can get through anything, including this pandemic and police brutality, with one another.

One evening in August, I went to my second meeting of the day, a celebration for a dear friend's twenty-third anniversary sober. She shared what a difficult year this has been - she lost her only son in November, 2019. She, her two speakers, and the vast majority of the seventy-two people at the meeting were African American. The topic was grief, how to transform grief into compassion and love. The first speaker had also stayed sober through losing her mother, a sibling, jobs. Each loss brought grief, suffering, loss. But, with the help of the fellowship, she survived, sober, by accepting powerlessness, (first over alcohol, then over almost everyone and everything else), finding Powers greater than herself to restore her to sanity, and turning her life over to the God of her understanding.

The second speaker, another good friend, has been the caregiver for her son who had been shot and paralyzed from the neck down for many years. She considers him her daily inspiration to live life as fully as possible, one day at a time. I remember at her own celebration a few years ago, her son was able to join us in a church hall on a ground floor where we could wheel in his chair from the ambulance. The joy we are able to share with one another in these moments was immeasurable.

I am deeply grateful that facing my own powerlessness over alcohol has led me to a world-wide fellowship of alcoholics and a powerful spiritual path to recovery and a new life. I would never have this many new African American and Latino friends without the rooms of recovery. Every single day, there are concrete actions I can take to nudge members into leadership and service roles, urge friends to tell their stories, sponsor newcomers and to continue to share their experience, strength and hope with all of us. It is truly the most welcoming and non-discriminating group I've experienced.

Regardless of color, economic status, gender, health, education, we all face an alcoholic death if we do not stick together, help one another as if our lives depended on unity. They do!

Healing Through Inventory : The Steps

1986

Where had that courageous woman gone who faced thirty-five years in federal prison? Who defied judges, the FBI and parole boards to have her baby in secret? I wanted her back, but without all the arrogance.

I wrote my first fourth step inventory in the mountains alone in 1986. After three days of writing and crying, listing my resentments, I began to see patterns of pride, self-centered fear, blame and shame in my actions and relationships. I came home from that weekend to find that my father had died. I was deeply grateful for every word I had written about my resentments toward him, every tear shed. I doubt that I would have been able to organize his sad, small funeral without the insights I got from my inventory. My heart had opened to forgive him for being exactly what I was - a suffering alcoholic. I doubt that anything he did to me was ever intended to do the harm it did. Yet harm was done. If I expected forgiveness, understanding and support from my son, to whom I had done harm, I had to forgive my father - and forgive myself. Make amends, real changes in my attitude and behavior.

2020

Today, I continue a form of inventory as part of my morning journaling. I can tell if something is nagging me, a tightness in the stomach, a lump in the throat, a memory of something I did or said that was sarcastic, boasting, unmindful. I write about it, plan to make amends quickly, pray for the courage I need.

Many of the ways I have done harm, have acted out my white privilege, have been rooted in those same habits of ignorance, fear, blindness, pride and arrogance.

Part of the process of writing this book has been doing a fourth step (a searching and fearless moral inventory) on my own racism!

- What harm have I done?
- How?
- When?
- To whom?
- How can I change?

As I look back on my life, some of these habits seem to stand out as patterns of racist thinking and action on my part:

- Blindness to and distancing from the suffering of others in my life.
- Complacency - resting on my laurels, on my past work.
- Trying to save the world, change racism on my own. Forgetting the need for community to effect real change.
- Pride, arrogance, self-righteous judgment of others.
- During my five-year relationship with an African American man, I learned a lot, but am sure I also made stupid remarks, offended his family with my drinking.
- One of the ways I harmed my son was by forcing him to make friends with Black children in the D.C. Unite to Fight Back. I had no right to choose his friends for birthday parties (some of which were disasters).

I want to be vigilant in seeing the patterns of white privilege in my life today, to listen to criticism from others and use my privileges to change this system of white supremacy into one that recognizes equality for all of us.

I call on my Irish blood ancestors and also my Native American and African American ancestors and activist teachers to give me direction. May they help me transform my negative, limited habit energies into courage, compassion and strong, loving, non-violent action. I always want to remain open to change and growth.

JUST MERCY

2020

I spent hours, one week, this summer absorbed in a powerful book - *Just Mercy* by Bryan Stevenson. This young Black lawyer tells the story of his work to obtain justice for people wrongly imprisoned, especially on death row in Alabama. He is a great example for me of learning not only from my ancestors but from younger activists today.

The main story is that of Walter McMillian, who spent six years on death row in Alabama for being Black. He not only didn't kill a girl he had never seen, wasn't a killer, had no criminal record at all, but he was with witnesses the entire day she was killed, including a white witness. It's a totally unjust story, using witnesses bribed or coerced by a judicial system motivated by race hatred and white supremacy at its boldest.

But a young African American lawyer persisted, reinvestigated his case, met with Walter and his family, filed endless appeals, until finally gaining justice for McMillian. The Equal Justice Initiative which he founded continues to take cases of death row inmates and fight for justice for many forgotten Black prisoners.

Several chapters are devoted to groups of prisoners whose numbers have vastly increased in the last thirty years in the US, the majority African American: women, children and the mentally ill.

I was moved by a heart-rending story about Trina, a 14-year-old girl in Pennsylvania, poor, severely abused, who accidentally started a fire that killed two boys. Condemned to life in prison without parole, she was raped by a prison guard and delivered his baby while handcuffed to a bed. Her child taken from her and placed in foster care. Exactly the fear I had for the child I carried when I walked into a courtroom to be sentenced on five federal felonies. I was horrified to read, "It wasn't until 2008 that most states abandoned the practice of shackling or handcuffing incarcerated women during delivery." (Stevenson, 2014, p. 151)

Unimaginable cruelty!

Ian, a 13-year-old, was convinced by older boys to participate in a robbery that resulted in a woman being wounded. Sentenced to life imprisonment without parole and he was sent to one of the toughest adult prisons in Florida. Since juveniles were five times more likely to be victims of sexual assault in prison, he spent 18 years in uninterrupted solitary confinement.

Stevenson explains that over 50% of prison and jail inmates in the US have a diagnosed mental illness, a rate nearly five times that of the general population. There are many stories of Black people locked up, imprisoned, and killed because their erratic behavior was not recognized as mental illness.

This summer we marked the first anniversary of the murder of a 23-year-old Black man, Elijah McClain in Aurora, CO. Waving his hands while listening to music, walking down the street near his home, he was stopped by police, either didn't hear or understand their commands, was wrestled to the ground, beaten, put in a choke hold, injected with ketamine, had a heart attack, and died. So far, none of the police officers have been indicted, arrested, or prosecuted for the murder.

The suffering of over 400 years of slavery, Jim Crow laws, lynching and systemic discrimination continues, overwhelms us.

In addition to his victories at winning stays of execution and freedom for death row inmates, Stevenson has a constant theme of hope in the possibility of changing entrenched racism, even in the deep South.

One of his stories I found moving was about a white guard on death row. When Stevenson first encountered him, the guard abused him verbally, and made him submit to a strip search, a practice never used for lawyers visiting clients. After several days of guarding one of Stevenson's mentally ill clients, Avery, in a court hearing, the guard experienced a change. Stevenson and his experts exposed the background of the prisoner as an abused foster child, suffering from severe, documented mental illness. When they were back at the prison, the guard confided in Stevenson that he had "come up in foster care" too, that he didn't think there was anyone who had it worse than he did. Listening to the hearing had shifted his heart. On the way back from the hearing to the prison, the guard had stopped to buy Avery the only thing he had been longing to have for months - a chocolate milkshake.

Change is possible, even in the most entrenched racist hearts and systems. No matter if it takes the rest of our lives, we must keep listening deeply to people's experience, connecting with them as equal human beings, and acting against injustice. We shall overcome!

Bryan Stevenson has an amazing legacy of accomplishments in fighting injustice in the US prison system. It's ridiculous to compare anything I've done to stop racism to this man who has dedicated his life to getting Black people (and others) off death row.

His amazing work humbles me, makes me wonder, as I do every day, what more I can do, being who I am, at this point late in my life, to effectively stop the insanity of racial oppression.

More Mercy, More Work to Do

Bryan Stevenson argued for prisoners before the Supreme Court five times, winning a case (Graham v. Florida) in 2010 that ruled life imprisonment without parole sentences imposed on children convicted of non-homicide crimes is cruel and unusual punishment. And in 2012, he won a constitutional ban (Miller v. Alabama) on mandatory life-without-parole sentences imposed on children convicted of homicides. Huge victories that helped overturn the sentences of thousands of people who would have died in prison otherwise.

His Equal Justice Initiative is definitely one cause I support! This tireless work, case after heart-breaking case, year after year, for over thirty years has also expanded into educational efforts.

I loved Stevenson's chapter 'Broken.' He admitted crying listening to Jimmy Dill trying to articulate his gratitude for EJI's efforts to save his life, moments before he was executed. All the lawyer's hard work failed this time to save a man who had been deprived and sexually abused as a child, had never received treatment for his many disabilities and had to be lifted from a wheelchair to his execution. It was a moment when Bryan felt defeated, overwhelmed by the senseless loss of life, the wrongness of it all. He wondered "Why am I doing this?"

His answer to himself is something we all need to hear:

"My years of struggling against inequality, abusive power, poverty, oppression and injustice had finally revealed something to me about myself. Being close to suffering, death, executions, and cruel punishments didn't just illuminate the brokenness of others, in a moment of anguish and heartbreak, it also exposed my own brokenness. You can't effectively fight abusive power, poverty, inequality, illness, oppression, or injustice and not be broken by it.

We are all broken by something. We have all hurt someone and have been hurt. We all share the condition of brokenness even if our brokenness is not equivalent. "I desperately wanted mercy for Jimmy Dill and would have done anything to create justice for him, but I couldn't pretend that his struggle was disconnected from my own…We are bodies of broken bones. I guess I'd always known but never fully considered that being broken is what makes us human… Our shared vulnerability and imperfection nurtures and sustains our capacity for compassion.

We have a choice. We can embrace our humanness, which means embracing our broken natures and the compassion that remains our best hope for healing. Or we can deny our brokenness, deny compassion, and, as a result, deny our own humanity (Stevenson, 2014,p.189)."

A deep look at my own brokenness happened when I reached my alcoholic bottom, that moment when I knew all my efforts alone to stop drinking were hopeless. I had failed in relationships, especially with my partner Jeff and my son. I had done the most harm to the people I loved most. I failed to bring about revolutionary change in our country, to stop Terrence Johnson from going to jail, to stop racial oppression that still happened every day. What was the use of continuing to struggle, continuing to try to heal, to stop myself and other broken people from doing so much harm to others?

I can still go back to those questions, those feelings of defeat and hopelessness at any given moment of difficulty or doubt. But to stay in despair for more than a few moments is certain death for me. The path of despair for me is the path back to drinking, to death.

So, I did what Bryan Stevenson did at his moment of despair. I reconnected with the people who inspired me with their lives to keep getting up, to keep my "eyes on the prize." Martin Luther King, Nelson Mandela, Rosa Parks, all my teachers and ancestors, young people in the Black Lives Matter movement. They reminded me to never let the vast brokenness, inhumanity and cruelty of the system appear larger in my mind and heart than the healing energy, love and compassion that abounds in our world.

If I have received mercy and forgiveness for the mistakes I made in the depths of my own suffering and weakness, then mercy and healing is available now, even for seemingly impossible changes in our lives, in our country, in the world.

I had to be brought very low, to a point of total surrender and powerlessness, to realize that the same despair, anger, and fear that was ruling my life was the emotional state that led to desperate acts. I knew I was capable of mistakes and passions that landed others on death row.

Bryan also thought about the executioners of Jimmy Dill, saw that they were broken people too, that their ignorance, fear, anger, and desire for revenge had created an entire deadly system of cruel punishments. Given different conditions and experiences in our lives, Bryan or I might be the ones making the judgment to sentence a person to death row or throw the electric switch to execute him. Healing for these people is as necessary as healing for their victims and healing for ourselves if we are to have true change in our racist system.

Bryan Stevenson concludes his powerful chapter with this insight:

"The power of just mercy is that it belongs to the undeserving. It's when mercy is least expected that it's most potent - strong enough to break the cycle of victimization and victimhood, retribution, and suffering. It has the power to heal the psychic harm and injuries that lead to aggression and violence, abuse of power, mass incarceration (Ibid, 294)."

He left his office that night broken and broken-hearted over the execution of Jimmy Dill but knew he would come back the next day. "There was more work to do."

Racists are broken too.

It's easy to see that the victims of our racist system of mass incarceration are broken, wounded, in deep need of long-term healing and support. Black people will always be in the forefront of the fight to end white supremacy, to change policies, laws and any forms of discrimination that are killing them. White people also need to do everything we possibly can to change the laws and policies, to stop the killing - because these same sick policies affect us too and because everyone benefits from an antiracist society.

What has been difficult for me to see is that the perpetrators of racism are also "broken," sick, wounded by white supremacy. What does it do to the guards locking people into isolation, beating, stunning, electrocuting, administering lethal injections to prisoners? To judges who order mandatory life sentences to children? To legislators whose "get tough on crime" laws result in the US having one quarter of the prisoners in the world? To the police who continue to maim and kill innocent Black people on the streets of this country?

Recently, Jacob Blake was shot in the back eight times by police while his three children watched from his car. Where does such misguided cruelty come from? How did white supremacists come to be so afraid, so hardened of heart?

Psychiatrists explain that "hurt people hurt people." Wounded and broken people wound and break others. Perhaps they don't know another way. Of course, whatever wounding has taken place to foster racism, the people, governments, and systems bear the responsibility not only to recognize harm done, change, enact just policies and laws, but also make reparations for past harms. We are responsible for our actions, and for the government that represents us.

Stamped from the Beginning

White supremacy that results in the mass incarceration and murder of Black people is not just the result of individual attitudes and habits; it is an entrenched system that affects every institution in our country. The best summary I've found of the development of that system and traces the struggles against it is Ibram X. Kendi's definitive history of racist ideas - *Stamped from the Beginning*. Kendi clearly demonstrates how, over 400 years in the US, racism keeps arising in new forms and new leaders, including assimilationists who assume white superiority in their plans and policies. As racism grows a new ugly approach, so new forms of antiracism must constantly be practiced countering it.

My Grandmother's Hands

Another powerful African American author and teacher, Resmaa Menakem, has been practicing domestic violence and trauma therapy for many years. In *My Grandmother's Hands*, he declares "white-body supremacy is in the air we breathe, the water we drink and the culture we share. We literally cannot avoid it. It is part of the operating system and organizing structure of American culture. It's always functioning in the background, often invisibly, in our institutions, our relationships and our interactions." (Menakem, My *Grandmother's Hands*, xix).

In his chapter, "European Trauma and the Invention of Whiteness," he maintains that white Americans inherited trauma since the 1500s that fostered white supremacy. Torture, cutting off of body parts, decapitation and public hanging for petty crimes numbed human empathy. Immigrants fleeing poverty, starvation, plague, imprisonment, and torture brought with them the brutal practices they passed on to slaves in this country.

Long before the concept of whiteness was coined in 16th century Portugal, whites practiced cruelty upon other white bodies. Then in the new world, this cruelty turned into genocide against the indigenous peoples who had lived here for many centuries, and to slaves brought forcibly from Africa.

Menakem maintains that white supremacy and the trauma it causes to both Black and white people must go deeper than changing thinking and structures in society. "White supremacy doesn't live in our thinking brains. It lives and breathes in our bodies." His experience is in therapy, and he offers workshops, meditations and healing practices not only for African Americans, but also for European Americans, particularly the military and police.

Interdependence

My life experience has taught me that although various groups have been segregated and discriminated against in our society, the end result is that we all suffer from the resulting inhumanity of one group against another. Racist thinking is dualistic, imagining separations and differences where they don't exist.

I didn't know about interdependence growing up. Interdependence, I have learned now, is that *all* things are interconnected with each other. Everything--the sun, the moon, the sky, the animals, the trees and plants, the air, the water-- all things are interconnected. We depend on them for existence. Our breath nourishes the plants and trees. We INTER-ARE.

I had to learn about our deep human interconnection, often from my own suffering. If we are to heal as a nation, the healing will benefit us all. Our humanity suffers when we do harm to others, no matter the reason.

No one is free when others are oppressed.

There were similarities between the early days of my recovery from alcoholism and my waking up to racism. Slowly it dawned on me, through hearing the stories of other people, that I had caused great harm during my active drinking years. There is a wonderful story in recovery literature about a man who came out of his bunker after a tornado, relieved that the wind had stopped blowing, saying to his wife, "Ain't that great, Ma, the wind's stopped blowin!" Unaware that he was the tornado in his family's lives.

Although in sobriety, I learned that I have a real physical/mental illness, I knew I was the one pouring alcohol into my body daily for at least the previous ten years. No one had forced me. I couldn't continue to blame my alcoholic father, my boyfriend and his friends, or my despair over the Reagan years. I was responsible for my actions, for the suffering I had caused, especially to my son. I had lots of work to do, much healing of myself and my relationships. I knew I would have the support on this journey with my powerful group of multinational friends in recovery.

The awakening to racism that began for me in 1963 in Montgomery, Alabama was similar. I felt overwhelmed at the depth of the suffering caused by white people, by people like me. George Wallace, the governor of Alabama, was cheering the use of dogs attacking school children protesting segregation. My own white students and their parents were so afraid of breaking with the system of racial oppression in Alabama that most refused to join an integrated Catholic school baseball team. And today, here, where I live, babies are incarcerated, and police are still killing Black people.

Using the steps to recovery from alcoholism is a life-long journey for me, as is the healing of our bodies and souls from the cruelties we cause to people of color every day.

Part of both journeys for me has been looking at my Irish-American ancestors, both their suffering from alcoholism and their collaboration in the systems of white supremacy. The process also involves appreciating the gifts of resilience and healing they offer us.

These approaches - Stevenson's work to stop mass incarceration and the death penalty, Menakem's to heal both the racist and the victims of racism, Kendi's relentless exposure of racism - are necessary.

My challenge now was to find the antiracist work that fit my experience, my life.

TEACHING/THE DIVERSITY WORKSHOP
1987-2007

D.C. 1987-1998

In the fall of 1986, after returning from an incredible cultural experience of living with a poor family for six weeks in Nicaragua to learn Spanish and understand their revolutionary society, it was time to find full-time employment. Did I mention that I lost that fancy television job when I was ten months sober? How could I continue activist work that fed my soul and be a sober, financially responsible parent at the same time?

Someone suggested I do the exercises in *What Color is Your Parachute* by Richard Bowles. One writing exercise involved describing five activities (not necessarily paid work) that I enjoyed, then list the skills related to the activities. I had so many red marks in the columns about teaching, that my next career path seemed obvious. It also happened to be the only one of the experiences that I could also conceivably be paid to do.

YES! My heart knew this was the right next step. I had wanted to teach since playing school at age four with my brother. I had loved teaching as a nun. I had tried to break into the D.C. Public Schools over the years of doing union organizing, so I had taken courses to qualify for a new teaching area - Social Studies.

If I expected to continue my activist work as a teacher, I wanted to be as free as possible to teach African American history, discuss current events, show good documentaries like *Eyes on the Prize* and make a real difference in the lives of students. Social Studies in the D.C. Public Schools required certification in thirty-two different subject areas, in addition to constantly added education requirements. Fortunately I loved to learn, so I would continue taking courses over the next twenty years of teaching in public high schools.

My big break came in a timely fashion. I had jumped through a number of certification hoops in D.C. by the time a possible job opened. I had spread the word among activist friends that I was looking for a teaching job and found a woman who was ready to transfer to a different school.

I remember being very nervous in my meeting with the principal, Michael Durso. I found out from a teacher friend that he was married to an African American woman and had several children in D.C. schools. He also had a reputation as a tough leader and a man of principle. One of the students at Wilson Senior High School had allegedly raped a female student in the school. Durso defied the school board's insistence that he allow the male student back in classes. He challenged the board; under threat of losing his job, he said, "No." He wouldn't permit the female student to be subjected to further harassment.

I felt I could work for a white man who operated on moral principles and had an intimate understanding of African American people. The D.C. schools were majority African American at this time, both students and teachers, in contrast to the surrounding suburbs which had majority white students and almost no African American teachers.

I got the job teaching World Problems, US Government and Advanced Placement Comparative Government in the International Studies Program! Fortunately the D.C. system never investigated my criminal record, so the five federal felonies were no obstacle on this job, as they would prove to be in the future.

The first day alone with five classes packed with students, taking attendance overwhelmed me, let alone trying to keep order and focus on content. In my first teaching career, being a nun had given me an authority that I didn't have here. I would have to gain every ounce of respect I got on my own with my students.

I was such an emotional mess by the end of that first day, that my son thought I had taken a drink. I babbled when I picked him up from his school. The rest of the semester was pretty rough, many of the students treating me like a "sub" rather than a full-time teacher, since I had arrived in February. Obviously, I wasn't Mrs. Friedman. Could I even be myself in this very stressful environment?

Learning from Students

My students were much more important to me than I was to them. They taught me every day. Most teenagers don't pay much attention to teachers, since we make them do so many things they think are stupid. Some definitely benefited by our time together. Many had life-changing experiences in the Diversity Workshop. Many became real friends, came to my wedding, are still in touch to this day.

Due largely to the support of great colleagues, a good principal and tolerant students, I didn't quit after that first horrible day in February 1987. I gradually learned how to plan lessons that stimulated good discussions and grade piles of homework and writing assignments. But I still felt like a substitute, and not much of one for the great teacher whose place I had taken.

The following September was very different. I had most of the summer free to read the textbooks, plan and dig up posters from my revolutionary days. I was fired up to teach the history that I had lived in the Civil Rights and anti-war eras. I had made some friends in the Social Studies and English departments who inspired and encouraged me.

I remember an African American gentleman who had taught one Advanced Placement English class to about thirty (usually all white) students every year. Together, over several years, we pushed to expand the AP classes to include more Black students. I remember many conversations with students urging them to take these "free" college courses. "Why not take advantage of them and qualify for college credit?" By the time I left Wilson SHS in 1998, we looked down from a window in the hallway by my classroom to an entire library full of majority African American students taking Advanced Placement exams. It felt like huge progress in just a few years.

Historically Wilson SHS had been a majority white school in the NW quadrant of D.C., the most affluent. By the early 80's, most D.C. schools were majority African American, including Wilson. An International Studies Program attracted students from other areas of D.C. and included students from the embassies in the neighborhood also.

One of the advantages of being part of the International Studies Program was the ability to design our own curriculum. My World Problems class, required for all tenth grade IPS students, shifted in content each year depending on current events. I usually began the course with a student-generated list of what they considered the most pressing issues in our city, country and world. The goal of the course was to examine as many of these issues as possible, often covering some through individual research and reports. Discussion was always lively on Racism, Domestic Violence, Gun

Control, Prisons/Death Penalty, War, Women's Issues, Drugs. This class was also broad enough in content that I was able to extend my research to visiting other countries, attending workshops and courses on a wide range of topics.

Teaching had become another in-depth experience for me of constantly learning more about my own white privilege and showing me ways to use it to empower young people. Every day my students convinced me more of their intelligence, creativity, curiosity, skills and power to change their world.

Children of Violence

In my early years teaching at Wilson, the homicide rate in D.C. was the highest in history. It coincided with a crack cocaine epidemic and an increase in incarceration of young Black men. The sale of cocaine was promoted by the Reagan administration's CIA to support the "Iran-Contra" war against Nicaragua (*CIA, contras, gangs, and crack*, 2014, p. xx) The Republican Congress also overturned D.C.'s strict gun laws, since we had no voting representation in that body. When I asked students if they knew a family member or neighbor who had been affected by gun violence, most hands in the rooms went up. Drugs? Again, up went the hands. The personal stories were heart-breaking - children woken up at night by gunfire, afraid to walk to the corner store, suffering wounds from drive-by shootings, losing friends, brothers, fathers to drugs, violence and prison.

My students and I looked at the history of these issues in D.C., the US and around the world. We researched, dug deeper than textbooks allowed, learned the truth about systematic racism in government policies on drugs, police, courts and prisons. We interviewed parents and grandparents about their memories of slavery in their families, went to the National Archives to research genealogy, invited guest speakers.

We organized demonstrations on gun violence and the government's involvement in drug trafficking in D.C.

We rallied when Terrence Johnson had yet another parole hearing.

We marched in front of the South African Embassy demanding the release from prison of Nelson Mandela.

We also made our classrooms safe places in which students could tell the truth about the real suffering in their lives. I encouraged journaling, something I had continued to do daily since my stay in the D.C. Women's Detention Center. I took the time to read my students' journals, giving them permission to mark pages not to read, and assuring them of complete confidentiality.

I remember one particular Haitian girl who was struggling with her genealogy project in US History class. She had journaled that she just couldn't do this project. She stayed after class one afternoon to tell me she had finally been able to find out information from her mother about her father. She wriggled in her seat, teared up but finally told me that she couldn't fill in the chart the "normal" way. I asked her why. "Because my grandfather is my father," she said. "He raped my mother when she was fifteen. She hates me because of that. I'm so embarrassed. I can't put it on the genealogy chart. I can't make an oral report like the others can. I don't know what to do."

I held her for a long time, let her sob into my shoulder.

Learning to Teach from my Students

The amount of suffering unleashed by my students when they felt comfortable sharing openly with me, in class or afterwards, was enormous. It completely changed my methods of teaching. I knew that they needed to learn US history, but might get a better sense of what history meant by learning their own history.

For my Haitian student, I couldn't change what happened to bring her into the world, but I could nourish her self-esteem, love her. Her mother shunned her most of her life, always aware that she was the child of incest, blamed the child. But she did have an aunt who loved and protected her most of her life.

In the next class on our genealogy project, I explained that the blood line chart provided by the Archives was only one approach to tracing our family history. Some of my African American students didn't know their great-grandparents; others had photos and rich stories back to slave times. But there they reached a huge problem; they found that the National Archives often listed numbers but not names of slaves. White slave masters were not listed as "father" for their Black children. More of the white students had family bibles listing ancestors, some back to colonial days. White privilege was laid bare in their own family histories.

Another student's work with the timeline of his life touched my heart. Even though his father had been born a sharecropper, he graduated from Fisk University and became a leader in the Civil Rights movement. He was mayor of D.C. when Chris was born. At age ten, Chris' father, the mayor, went to jail on drug charges and his parents split up, very publicly. I understood why this handsome sophomore dealt with the constant teasing by becoming the class clown. Tragedies and resilience abounded in every class.

So we also created "genealogy charts" that traced the reality of family structure for each child. Who "mothered" you and played the role of mother in your life? Who was a substitute grandmother, cousin, niece? I knew that it had been common among Jeff's family members and friends to have many cousins and aunts who bore no blood relationship. These were real family members, who showed up for holiday feasts, births, funerals. They needed to count, so each young person could claim not only a blood ancestry but a "love" ancestry. The results were varied, colorful drawings of trees, flowers, mazes, whatever picture most clearly demonstrated these important relationships in each person's life.

Today I couldn't possibly make a genealogy of my family that didn't include my daughter-in-love who still has her wonderful Cambodian mother, but is my daughter also.

The Diversity Workshop

The Diversity Workshop (DW) became my main passion outside regular classes throughout the remaining years of my second twenty-year teaching career, eleven years at Wilson SHS in D.C. and nine at Montgomery Blair HS in MD.

We developed our own version of a workshop I was trained to teach by NCBI (the National Coalition Building Institute). Having experienced many types of racism workshops over the years, I found this one the best for allowing open sharing of stories about real experiences of stereotyping and abuse without finger-pointing and guilt. It allowed everyone, of all ethnicities, religions, genders to celebrate the groups to which they belong, listen to one another's suffering and learn ways to interrupt racist jokes, slurs and actions, to become an antiracist.

What You Can't Tell Just by Looking at Me!

'Speak-outs' and 'Hidden Identities' became very important separate exercises for the high school students. They were fascinated by all they learned about one another when they told their own stories of stereotyping and discrimination or simply asked to name "Three things you can't tell just by looking at me." As our student leaders became more familiar with the power of their own stories, they might share Hidden Identities like this - "Hi, I'm Noah. Three things you can't tell just by looking at me - I'm gay, homeless, and a great saxophone player." Or "Hi, I'm Sabrina. I was born in Cameroon, am here illegally, and have stage three lymphoma." In the Speak-Outs, individuals were given the full attention of the whole group to listen deeply to their experience at length, without comment, just huge support.

We eventually learned a great deal about each student's "Hidden Identities," particularly difficult conflicts and the ways in which they had learned to stand up for themselves and become allies to others. Leaders emerged whose lives embodied several identities and became powerful examples of conflict resolution and leadership. One leader was open about his identities as a homeless, bisexual child of a drug addict. Another great leader was Indian, heterosexual, a brilliant female student being forced into an arranged marriage with a man she didn't know rather than go to college.

Building Peaceable Schools

After a couple of years of building the Diversity Workshop program at Wilson, other teachers became more involved and together we were able to create a "Peaceable Schools Program." A teacher, passionate about Peer Mediation, got permission from Dr. Bonner (then our African American female principal) to create a course training students to conduct mediation for conflicts between students, students and teachers, students and parents. Those teachers were called to divert conflicts and fights rather than police.

Another popular course was Peace Studies. Colman McCarthy had written several books full of readings on peace (by Gandhi, Martin Luther King, Jr, Thomas Merton, Nelson Mandela, Dorothy Day, etc). He ran a school training young people to teach Peace Studies courses as an elective in the DCPS and eventually in MCPS for credit. Students saw this course as a way to take the discussion of individual suffering from racism, sexism and an oppressive white supremacist system to the world level.

Our work at Wilson with the Diversity Workshop, Peace Studies and Peer Mediation eventually linked to American University's International Peace and Conflict Resolution Masters' Program. The college campus was near Wilson, so our teachers were able to take free classes at AU, and graduate students came to Wilson to practice-teach and receive Diversity Workshop training from our high school students. Wonderful trips abroad and opportunities to develop curriculum based on conflict resolution in Oman, Mexico, El Salvador and other countries also resulted.

The Peaceable Schools program was at its peak when I found it necessary to move to a different school system.

Teaching at Montgomery Blair HS in MD

1998-2007

There had been many times I was ready to quit the D.C. Public School system, always because of the system, not our school or our students. The lack of funding, the games played on us teachers due to racism in Congress, the dysfunction of the school board, (the only elected political office in D.C. for years) wore down one's soul. So, every year, I checked my status in surrounding school systems to make sure I was certified, should the conditions become intolerable. D.C. teachers received no Social Security benefits, so I knew I had to work somewhere else before retirement.

The chairperson of the Social Studies Department at Blair was particularly eager to have me join the Blair team because of my experience organizing the Diversity Workshop. The schedule first semester, moving to different classrooms and computerized grading were huge challenges I met with the support of fantastic colleagues. I remember Gibb gave me his entire notebook for African American History chocked full of great book lists, lesson plans and ideas.

Computers and whiteboard technology were available for every classroom. I had moved from a technical desert in D.C. to an abundant oasis in one of the richest counties in the country. Talk about white privilege! A main attraction for me was that Blair, the largest public high school in the state, had one of the most diverse student bodies.

As usual, it was the students who won me over with their enthusiasm, creativity and passion for social change. With strong department and administrative support, we held our first Diversity Workshop in the fall of 1998, trained new leaders, and built the program into a required activity for all 10th grade English/Social Studies teamed classes. I was also allowed to design and teach my curriculum for Conflict Resolution classes and Peace Studies, both of which took the lessons of the Diversity Workshop to a much deeper level.

9/11

I was teaching a Peace Studies class on September 11, 2001, when a student stopped at the door and hollered, "Turn on the TV! NOW!" We had difficulty with the news channel, so our class quickly moved to the library's big screen TV. We stood close to one another, watching together as the second plane hit the Twin Towers. I held two of the girls who were shaking, in tears as it was announced that another plane was headed for D.C.. So many of our students had parents who worked in downtown D.C. that they pulled out phones and began to dial them. Others asked if they could fetch younger brothers and sisters. I gathered all the students together in a huddle. We took deep breaths, looked one another in the eye. I said, "We don't have clear information yet, but whatever we do, let's try to stay calm. We're students of peace. What can we do right now to help?"

"Let's go to the office to make an announcement that will help keep order. I'll do it!,"" the Student Council president volunteered.

"Let's make sure we're calm enough, then spread out to help the younger students contact parents."

"Let's pray."

"Whatever we do, keep breathing," said one of the girls who meditated. "Right now, we're ok. "

LISTENING TO MY DIVERSITY WORKSHOP STUDENTS

2020

The Diversity Workshop was probably the most real, long-term, effective work that I did to educate, open hearts and minds to the realities of racism and sexism within us and in our society. I want the voices of my former students to speak for themselves about how the Diversity Workshop affected their lives, helped them tell their stories, speak up, stop oppression, become better leaders, make changes in our world. I know that it was an unending source of awareness of my own deep training in white privilege.

A constant 'WAKE UP' to reality, and invitation to keep growing, changing and listening for the rest of my life.

In September 2020, after months of daily writing on this book, I gathered several of my former Diversity Workshop leaders together on zoom to share about the experience of being a workshop leader in high school and to share what was happening in their lives today. The group is diverse - gay, lesbian, heterosexual; African American, white, Latina, Indian, Caribbean; unemployed, employed; some parents, some not; some in committed relationships, some not at this time; some religious, some not so much. I will let them speak for themselves about the impact of the Diversity Workshop on their lives.

LILAH (Blair '04)

I'm an artist in NY and just released my first album last year. I've also done some acting, directing, and events' coordinating. But there aren't many events happening with Covid, which hit New York so hard. So, I'm not working now. I am active in the health and wellness and spiritual communities in New York, and I hold a women's spiritual support group.

How did the Diversity Workshop NOT affect me?

I think about it all the time.

In college I strayed away, but this year especially with all that's going on, I think about it all the time. It's such a gift to have those conversations at such a young age. It shaped my way of thinking about the world so young - my openness and compassion toward problems in the world. I see the contrast with my friends here who didn't have that experience and can see it now as they have conversations with their families and become open about diversity. They just didn't have the exposure to the world and grew up in more homogeneous neighborhoods.

I grew up in Takoma Park which has so much diversity and laid the groundwork for relationships with many of my friends here in NY. There are so many protests here that we think about race and these issues all the time now. The DW helped me bring a lot of strength and knowledge to my conversations now.

Recently I had a friend ask, "Why are you so comfortable having conversations about race?" I began, "Let me tell you a story about the Diversity Workshop in high school."

I've been thinking a lot about the Diversity Workshop and reflecting on what I learned from my experiences in the program. I keep circling back to this one fundamental lesson, which is that you never know what the person sitting next to you is going through. We all suffer because we're all human. We've all lived through pain, grief, and loss. There's so much more to a person than a collection of societal stereotypes. There's so much more to learn and to feel when we connect with someone without projecting our assumptions onto them about who they are and what kind of life they have. It was an experiential lesson in compassion that became a central part of my belief system as I got older.

The Diversity Workshop was special because it gave teenagers something they desperately needed - a community of friends bonded through shared experiences that also celebrated what made each leader a unique individual. I've never heard of any other high school program quite like it.

SARAH (Blair '06)

I went to college in New York. Moved to Philly just before Covid. My wife and I have a newborn, a couple months old.

I feel very connected to the Jewish community in West Philly. It's fun being a parent. It's harder on my body than I expected... exhausting... I'm doing all of our laundry and the baby's every other day! There are thousands of things to do! But they're already smiling, cooing. That's the big news here!

I work for a Jewish environmental non-profit. I do administration, texting, dealing with technology, managing their data base. Before Covid, the center held retreats. The staff are all white Jews in the retreat center, but the kitchen staff are all Black and Latino.

We applied for a grant to do diversity training at the retreat center, but now that we're shut down due to Covid, we're doing it among the staff. We're getting to really know one another, asking where folks came from, how they are feeling in this political movement, asking questions, listening, trying to have real conversations.

I've been struck by how little experience they have with this. I've thought about all of these things. I've been so involved in political stuff for years that I'm almost exhausted by it.

But these folks on the staff, most in their mid-30s just haven't thought about racism, about their own privileges, their own ways they've been included or excluded.

I've been blown away. These conversations have helped me appreciate what I'm able to bring to it - comfort asking questions, redirecting us to something more generous or meaningful.

I realize how these skills started back in high school. They helped me become a really good facilitator, but they also helped me explore and reveal my own identity as a gay woman.

Conversations around race and sexuality, beginning to have a vision of life, really started in the Diversity Workshop. It helped me loosen up and be comfortable with where life might go, what might happen. It prepared me for the unprepared and I'm totally grateful for that.

DAVID   (Wilson SHS '96)

The Wilson SHS Diversity Workshop was really directional for the rest of my life! Meeting a former nun who had raided Dow Chemical's offices was definitely special. She was also the first person who got me to read the Communist Manifesto. So, I squeezed some discombobulated pieces of Marxism into my speech at our high school graduation.

I was also a Wilson Player, the drama club with Sameena here. I went to NYC where I could dance a lot - to Columbia U which was near the Alvin Ailey dance studio.

I also met a group espousing the Communist Manifesto and spent twelve and a half years in the group, didn't finish my degree at Columbia, didn't get a PhD because of it (very like Joann's story of education in NYC that we shared one time when she visited me at the MOMA. We never did see the exhibit, did we?).

In NY the police brutality issues pulled me into political action - especially supporting the Haitian Abner Louima raped with a toilet plunger in the Brooklyn police station in '97. I had dealt with anti-Blackness all my life.

I wish there had been more of a class analysis embedded in the workshop. There were wealthy parents supervising the DW, and it made them feel really good. But at the end of the DW, I felt there were things we were missing about power and transformation. If you do feel so good living here in 'Western Caucasia,' what do you need to do with your wealth to actualize a vision of liberation!

So for a while, I was in a willful, egotistical space where my conception of anti-racism was right. And I no longer hold that view, am not sure what I do think my role is in the movement world, moving forward. I've been an organizer all my life. In

D.C. with Casa de Maryland. I was their anti-racism organizer and educator for a couple of years. They had funding from the Ford Foundation! The Ford Foundation was paying me to do that work.

This is the super-cool project, bringing us together now. You had people going through that framework of looking at and unpacking oppression and liberation in high school! It totally opened me up to other possibilities. Even when I had criticisms in my mind, I never stopped thinking about it.

I've been in some accountability issues in movement spaces I've been in. Also dealing with mental health issues. So now I'm focusing on recovery constantly and also working on other compulsions. And I'm in a Social Work Masters' Program. Dealing with recovery during Covid, I realized that I need qualifications to really support myself! It's going well. I had no idea how to pay for school, but a grant appeared to cover it!

It's so great to be with people here I've known since I was 14!

SAMEENA (Wilson SHS '95) Anthropology Professor

Some things that Sarah said, I really resonated with - and David, OMG!

I've lived in Wisconsin since before the '08 election. I'm an anthropology professor at a Jesuit university. It's really good to see you all. I graduated from Wilson in 1995 and went to the U of

MD at College Park. David's mom said I was ruining my life to go to a public school. I got into some Ivys, but got a full ride at MD.

David - Did my mom really say that? She's only supposed to talk to me like that!

Sameena - They loved us too hard, and that love comes at a bitter, bitter price. She meant well, but I'm glad I went to MD, then to the New School in NY for 12 years. So David and I got to hang out a bit there. I think I visited you in Central Harlem and Sugar Hill.

Then I went to Baltimore for my PhD, so I've always lived in cities. It's not just the Wilson/ Diversity Workshop that shaped me, but it's also a D.C. thing that made a difference.

Living now in Milwaukee, I'm experiencing one of the most segregated cities in the country. It hurts my heart every day that Milwaukee has never had a Black mayor. There's a Black majority but no Black mayor!

People here think that if you don't speak English well you're not educated. In D.C. you can't make those assumptions about people - about language or class background. That guy might be a Pakistani diplomat or work for Voice of America. You just never know.

I have a reputation for being good at dealing with difficult people and having difficult conversations. I'm an anthropology professor. I teach a course about Ethno-centrism and Antiracism. But all my research is on gender-based violence, sexual assault, interventions in hospitals and courts. So it's been this additional journey of dealing with the carceral feminist in me that thinks prisons are NOT the answer, that we need to get rid of them….to prevent or transform the violence against women. They don't work!

Thank you, Angela Davis!

I'm done with that. I've also written about masculinity, the nexus of vulnerability in gender-based violence and killings by police.

It's hard. I've put myself in a setting where I have a front seat, not just as an observer, but a participant, with a stake in all the research I do. I'm not just an observer. I didn't become an anthropologist just to watch people suffer. My first big project was at a rape crisis center in Baltimore. There's just a lot of racist shit that runs through the medical system. It's not an accident; it's a feature!

And I just finished a big study on the courts. What happens when you go to court for justice? You get screwed! The racist, sexist narratives about Black women and the anti-masculine narratives about Black men and Latino men in courts! I'm ready to burn the whole thing down!

I'm working in a white university, not just predominantly white. Those white dudes in the administration resent People of Color!

Everyone wants me to fix their problems, but everyone also hates me for it.

I just exist in this space of, "What the hell am I doing here? I want to go HOME"…but this is my home now. It's where I am. So, yeah.

BRETTNEY (Blair '08)

"I'm at the Wharf in D.C. right now. I live in MD now. Was in LA for a year and did a bunch of different jobs there, worked in a Women's and Children's Shelter for victims of domestic violence.

Now, I work in Silver Spring at my parents' home healthcare facility. I'm their Human Resources Director. It's a medium sized business but growing. I go to church in NE D.C., Grace Covenant, and am really involved with the students and young adult groups there.

I'm also working on my fashion brand and label, launching it in early 2021. Would love to get together with more Diversity leaders!

KATHRYN (Blair '04)

At the moment I'm an unemployed art teacher, but also a visual/performance artist who is building a website to give artists a place to sell their works now that doing so on the streets is impossible with Covid.

I identify as unemployed. I worked in New Orleans for ten years in a private charter school, K-2, as a visual arts teacher.

I hear what Sameena is saying about how segregated cities are. Most of the schools in New Orleans have Black and Brown kids taught by white teachers. Teachers like me who are inexperienced. The kids are taught to comply, not to think critically, to ask questions. I miss New Orleans, but it's nice to be back in a diverse place like D.C./Silver Spring. I live in a neighborhood where the lower income renters are being pushed out and houses sold to wealthy people (white people). It seems like every conversation I've had since May devolves into anger.

What I tell folks about the Diversity Workshop is that after two days of a workshop, I went away thinking, "Dang, we all have so much in common! We're all the SAME! We HURT! WE FEEL FEELINGS! Every kid feels alone. And maybe being at a big school on the beltway of D.C. the Diversity Workshop helped me feel less alone.

I walked away from the Diversity Workshop with a lot of tools, skills for listening and talking to people who don't look like me….or think like me or have the same background as me.

As an adult, all the diversity, equality and inclusion training I've attended involved a lot of being talked AT, given DATA, told "You've gotta think this way." And I think that the power of allowing children to TALK to one another openly and giving them the TOOLS, the parameters of a safe space to do so is LIFE-

CHANGING!!! Kids need to be humans, to start early to understand one another.

Thank you for bringing us together - back in high school and now.

Maria (Blair '07)

Avi and I were co-presidents of DW the last year (when we graduated and you left, 2007). I did DW three years and we took it to different schools, did a LOT! Thought we were making an impact. We had no words back then for white privilege or microaggressions which we've learned since, have evolved. What we did learn is still very familiar.

After Blair, I went to the U of Md and lived in D.C.. First, I studied Psychology, then Sociology because I thought the environmental factors were missing. When I went to the University of Maryland, it was strange to be around so many white people, which is crazy - because my entire upbringing was so diverse, growing up in Silver Spring. Every school I went to had every culture and nationality. How amazing it is to grow up around so many cultures, where it's normal to be around so many different languages, traditions, values. We became open and accepting of diversity.

Now I work in a very segregated city. I work at a center for child and family traumatic stress. I work with families in the area, mostly Black or Latino. We do a lot of evidence-based treatment.

I use art in expressive therapy treatment with my kids. If someone has experienced trauma, it impacts one's ability to communicate clearly. And expressive art allows the brain to rewire and find new ways to communicate. I really love my work.

My role with DW really brought me into this work where I can help people, make real changes for those who are marginalized and disturbed. We are struggling for equality on the job where there is so much discrimination and unfairness. People of color have to work twice as hard and get less for it. I'm at the bottom of the totem pole to make changes. That's frustrating. The people who hold power don't want change.

Interjection: **Katie** - "Argh, why aren't you the boss."

It's a lot of emotional labor. At least I'm happy I'm part of a group that has those desires for change. We need leaders in the summit group capable of change, and it's frustrating. I feel the pain of the world as a trauma therapist. With the pandemic, we have to work with more patients. Working at home sucks, violates my sanctuary. But that's what's going on.

J M – "Being on the front lines is tough…thank you for doing it."

Sameena - "It's SO hard to change institutional racism!"

We're trying to get our institution to make real changes. Beyond just being known as an antiracist is a step.

AVI S (Blair '07)

Last time I saw you was on the University of MD campus. DW is definitely a linchpin, core moment in my life.

I dropped out of the CAP (Communications Arts Program) at Blair, a very competitive program which felt very clique-y, a competition for who could be the same person. Then there was an incident with someone harassing a CAP person in the bathroom and we did a DW for the whole CAP program. I said, "WOW, who are these people! I want to be part of this. This is awesome!"

I can relate to everyone here. All the walls came down in that workshop! Even though it did feel like competition among all the clique-y people about who suffered the most. During Hidden Identities especially. I walked into 10th grade CAP the next fall and said, "I don't want to be here." So I dropped it. I said I want to be in the classes Ms. Malone teaches, so I took her Sociology class.

But in terms of what it really brought me - I reference the DW all the time. I'm teaching high school now and some of the kids feel that they have to join everything for their Resume. I tell them, find something you're really passionate about and DO THAT!

Do you remember the Identity Projects? People would talk about their identity and I did one on Gay Parents. (Avi has six parents, his gay moms and his four gay and bisexual dads, two African American).

Another did one on poetry. In that workshop, I wrote my first poem as a result. Then started writing songs, created a studio out of my dorm room in college, recording songs for my classes, now teaching my students how to do the same. We won the WAMMIE (Washington Area Music Award) this summer. And I went on to get a Masters in Audio Production and Engineering!

That was one area that led to the rest of what I'm up to.

In college, I learned about tracking as an institution. It led me to History of Education and ultimately get a Masters in education. I enjoyed DW, and being an RA, also counseling. We did a DW for my floor in college…which led me to involvement in equity issues there and a desire to keep teaching. DW set in motion what has become the rest of my career.

You talked about white privilege and micro-aggressions. I remember "First Thoughts" put those issues out there clearly - without the terms. I love terms like these and "woke" and "antiracism."

Kids in my high school say, "There's so much diversity here." And I say, 'It's so WHITE!!!" I've traveled a lot but there's no place quite as diverse as D.C./Silver Spring. When I go away, the kids say, "You'll be back!"

I have a test when I travel looking in restaurants at who's sitting near one another, who is the wait staff, the owners.

Not many cities pass the test - Salt Lake City did. But Milwaukee and New Orleans, not at all. Very segregated.

Went to Washington University in St. Louis for grad school, took the first teaching job at Germantown, MD. The first year I didn't meet standards. I almost didn't succeed. It was really tough. I think it was my third year when you came to do the DW with my class, and by then I felt more solid. In fifth year, I became the Coordinator of the Academy of Bio-technology. I've taught nine different courses, including Music Technology, Chemistry, Molecular Biotechnology. This is my ninth year now, I can hardly believe it.

We were working to reduce tracking here, so they made all the classes "honor" classes. Now there are more heterogenous classes. Before, though it seemed the teachers were recommending the students fairly, the students weren't placing themselves in the higher level classes. It was like the internalized oppression exercise in the DW.

There is so much resistance from teachers. "We're dumbing down the curriculum!" But the curriculum wasn't really fair to start with.

Now teaching virtually we have four hours a week instruction in a subject instead of six hours. But we've really 'over-densified' the content over the years, so they probably really were having too much.

I also have a club that started for a musical, when I made back-up tapes in case someone got sick. The kids asked for a class to learn how to do that.

I asked Ms Malone, "How do you attract people to a club, make it grow?"

She told me what I now tell my students - "Pick something you're passionate about, join with people who love to do it too. Share what you produce! Others will come."

RACISM is a job for WHITE PEOPLE to clean up!

TERRENCE (Wilson SHS '99)

I grew up in D.C., sometimes bullied, sometimes popular, confused about relationships. I graduated from Wilson SHS in '99, am in my late 30's now, with a Masters in "Organizational Development" and a job with the D.C. Government.

"I had the all-American high school experience in the middle of a bubble." Wilson over-prepared me for college. I went to Seton Hall in Pittsburgh, formerly an all-white girls' Catholic school that had about thirty males at the time. Going to a workshop there on rape in the first few weeks was a challenge. I was suddenly the enemy when I had usually been the one bullied, excluded and isolated as a Black gay man. I could challenge inappropriate assumptions and ask, "Does violence only happen to women?"

Back in D.C., perhaps the only place I feel safe, I encountered unhelpful forms of political correctness. Some job rules on "3rd party uncomfortableness" were a bit over the top. For instance, when a person comes upon two men hugging in the hallway and is offended, is that "third party sexual harassment"? I also took offense at terms like "MY supervisor," saying, "NO! There is no 'MY' as a descriptor of YOU! No! My humanity doesn't belong to you. You don't own me!"

"When I lost my artistic side, I lost my voice."

"I can't do that to myself. I can't be quiet."

"I've been bullied. When I watched the scene in the film *When They See Us* where the boys "walked the neighborhood," I saw myself. We did that in D.C.! It was a thing in the '90s. I saw myself in the guy thrown in jail for nothing. He came to the station to support his friend and ended up in solitary for 16 years! For a rape he didn't commit!

I remember well being a Diversity Workshop leader, learning a lot about myself. It was great. I learned to speak out when I heard slurs and racist, homophobic remarks. The Peer Mediation training helped me mediate conflicts between friends. I loved being able to discuss O.J. Simpson's trial and hear different views. I used the DW model at Seton as a way to open up their limited focus on just women's issues. The DW allowed me to challenge inappropriateness.

Here are my recommendations - read *What Truth Sounds Like* by Michael Eric Dyson (conversations with James Baldwin, Robert Kennedy and others on racism). Listen to T. J. Jacks' podcast where he defines the difference between "constituents," "comrades," and "confidants" (the latter being the only category who loves you unconditionally).

We expressed gratitude that we still felt that bond of "confidant" after so many years apart.

When it came to "what to do now," he said that "RACISM is a job for white people to clean up!" We have to face reality. Face the truth. It will take lots of energy to dismantle this racist system. Make reparations. Stop the police murders of African Americans. All these years Black people have been screaming for ACTION! Do something! NOW!! VOTE!!! Change the government! change police departments! Change the justice system!"

VITAL (Blair '04)

Another afternoon was devoted to an interview/reunion on zoom with a wonderful former student leader of the Diversity Workshop. Vital is the survivor of two genocidal attacks in Rwanda. He was an exceptionally gifted, resilient, open person who shared the trauma he and his family experienced not only in our high school but in talks he gave at American University, the University of Pennsylvania and the US Institute of Peace as a teenager. Later in college, he was asked to speak at Berkeley, Brown and Northwestern universities about the genocide in Rwanda and conflict resolution.

He took his experience with the Diversity Workshop to a Quaker college where he helped form an inclusion initiative. He encountered disappointments in the college's reaction to Palestinian students from a Ramala Friend's school being beaten up by fifteen members of the football team. The racism and violence he suffered in Rwanda was also alive, even in a college that purported to be inclusive and peace-oriented in its philosophy.

He added, "There were other incidents targeting LGBT students, Black students, Native Americans, Hispanic and Latino students by the time we would conclude the drafting of our portion of the diversity plan. But at a higher level when I became Senate president, I realized that racism was built into the structure of the school consciously and unconsciously."

"More stories were teased out by other Multicultural Leadership Scholars and eventually culminated in an Antiracism training for the board itself. I loved that group in the Department of Multicultural Ed. It reminded me of the Diversity Workshop all over again, and the stakes were so high. They still are, and I wish there could be several required trainings for presidents, senators, judges, and Congressmen/women. Can you imagine a training for them like the one almost all tenth graders at Blair attended? Or even to require such training before becoming a public servant. It would change this world quickly.

Gosh it's just an inspiration to share with you!"

We discussed at length the question of how to heal the trauma of racism, sexism and class conflict, especially in family relationships.

I'm happy I'll have time to include his story in this book! And delighted to be re-connected to one of my favorite students. He is still teaching me!

MORE TEACHERS ON ANTIRACISM

Black Writers

How could I introduce my students to some of the same powerful African-America writers who had so influenced my viewpoint on racism? English was my primary teaching subject for the six years I taught as a nun, so I integrated as much Black literature and history as possible into all those classes. I introduced Phyllis Wheatley and Langston Hughes into classes on poetry, and novels by Maya Angelou, Alice Walker and Toni Morrison into American Literature. But teaching Social Studies allowed me to use almost any African American writers I wished, including Malcolm X, Bobby Seale, Ericka Huggins and Nelson Mandela. I also took suggestions from my students to add to extensive reading lists for every class.

2020

This summer, as I began writing this book, I reached out to my granddaughter for suggestions of books to read, films to see, organizations to which to donate. These are some of the reflections on some of my favorite authors and speakers in the last six months of intense study:

Ibram Kendi, *Stamped from the Beginning* and *How to be an Antiracist*

If you are looking for a definitive history of how the US developed into a white supremacist system, the best book I've read is Ibram Kendi's *Stamped from the Beginning.* He carefully traces the origins of racist ideas back to Greek and Roman justifications for slavery, depictions of Africans (disregarding ancient civilizations of Egypt, Ethiopia, Ghana, Mali and Songhay) as less than human. Gathering the history in the US around Cotton Mather, Thomas Jefferson, William Lloyd Garrison, W.E. B. DuBois and Angela Davis, he demonstrates the persistence of racism in using religion, law, institutions and policies to economically exploit people of color and extend violence and murder of African Americans to this day.

His *How to Be an Antiracist* is a shorter, beautifully argued and persuasive roadmap of how we can become antiracist, not only in thought but in action, how we can build an antiracist world "in all its imperfect beauty."

In Chapter 11, he convinced me that Black racism is possible! I had thought in the '60's it was racist to call Black people racist because it was whites that had the white supremacist POWER, that racism was "power over" others rather than "power with" others.

Anyone can think and act in either racist or antiracist ways, and individuals change all the time. I've changed, still change daily and must keep an open mind to keep learning how to be an antiracist. After all these years of trying to keep my feet on the path of antiracism, I have a long way to go to become entirely "woke."

What Kendi slowly, carefully proved in the chapter "Black" was that some African Americans have achieved great power - Clarence Thomas, judges, police chiefs, billionaires, and others have the choice to use that power in either a racist or antiracist way. An important example he gave was that of Ken Blackwell, Ohio's African American Secretary of State in 2004. He directed county boards to limit voters' access to the provisional ballots (in predominantly African American areas) that ensured people improperly purged from the voting rolls could vote. The effect of his action was to keep 174,000 potential votes from being cast, more than the number who re-elected Bush as president. Proof that an African American can commit racist actions.

So, it's not so black and white. Kendi calls this "powerless defense" the "illusory, concealing, disempowering and racist idea that black people can't be racist because Black people don't have power." This view was a huge shift in thinking for me, and I want to reflect similar shifts in my own history of political activism.

My tendency, my default still is to think in dualistic black and white opposites, either/or, good/bad. Mindfulness meditation has been the most effective practice to break into that thinking, to reveal its errors, to convince me that we "inter-are." I didn't have that understanding back in the late sixties when I had a platform to speak, the opportunity to help connect people around the country.

I was still motivated by the core of Christianity, the notion of love, but along with that valuable principle, I carried the baggage of a philosophy based on opposite extremes. When you are taught as a toddler that doing something "bad" can send you to hell forever, the fear is deep in the body, mind and emotions. I was motivated to be a good person, to do right, to stand up for my principles in the face of death, like Jesus and the martyrs. I didn't always succeed, had confession to fall back on, to hit a restart button, but I wanted to be a good person.

For the first twenty-two years of my life, I probably wasn't such a bad person, but I was an unwitting racist. I didn't know Black people, their suffering, didn't know that my skin color brought privileges even to a poor, working class girl. I began to see class privilege in high school, realizing that others had more money, more opportunities for education and career than I. But I didn't know that millions of African American people were prevented from the level of security that my family had.

Once my eyes were opened on a deep personal level in Alabama, I've had no excuse for any time I saw a person or situation from the vantage of white supremacy or acted in a racist manner. Part of the purpose for this book is to look more deeply at my own history and actions, to understand the subtle and insidious nature of racism, to be open to criticism of my actions and to demonstrate that white people like me can CHANGE.

Deciding to do the Dow action would, I knew, change the view that some people had of my goodness. I would lose their respect and have a difficult time explaining the purpose of our action. But I was convinced that it was the right thing to do, that the action took a stand against war, racism and capitalism. I still do, not that I ever felt the need to repeat that exact type of action. At the time it was the right thing for me to do.

I suppose that joining the action in my mind crossed a line of good and evil. I would never hold a government job or run for political office because of my felonies. I knew I was still capable of being selfish, egotistical, defensive, capable of making stupid mistakes, drinking; but I didn't think I could be racist, imperialist or war-mongering ever again. I was still rooted in dualistic, either-or thinking.

If Black people can be racists, I can still be racist. If I want to root out racism in my thinking and actions, I have to be constantly open to listen, to connect to people who are suffering from racism and to ACT constantly against injustice.

I think Kendi would agree that we can ACT in racist ways, no matter who we are, what we think or what we've done in the past.

He would say that we have to constantly look at actions, ours and those of others. White supremacy doesn't let go of power easily and is constantly shifting, re-appearing in new forms. We definitely see its strength in the present administration, in the millions who support "Making America White Again." I would hope that the January 6 attack on the US Capitol might be the last hurrah of white supremacy, but it might not die in my lifetime.

Kendi says, "Race is a mirage but one that we do well to see, while never forgetting it is a mirage, never forgetting that it's the powerful light of racist power that makes the mirage." (Kendi, *Antiracist*).

The reality is that we live in a world now with a majority people of color, a rich, diverse world. Rather than live in fear of losing what was never a culture of equality and appreciation of diversity, why not celebrate the wealth of the people of this world? Build truly diverse beloved communities?

AFRICAN-AMERICAN HEROES INSPIRE US

The spring, summer and fall of 2020 was consumed by fierce competition for the presidential elections and the loss of some great heroes of the struggles against racism and injustice, especially John Lewis and Ruth Bader Ginsberg. They continue to transmit courage to speak out against injustice and to celebrate all cultures, colors, all people in our society.

John Lewis

John Lewis died Friday, July 17, of pancreatic cancer. He was less than a year older than I am. I have followed his career standing for racial justice most of my life, admired him and consider him a great role model.

His non-violent protests began at age 17 and continued throughout his life, the last 33 years as a US congressman from Georgia. He met Martin Luther King at 18, integrated lunch counters as a Fisk University student in Nashville, suffered injuries to his face and ribs as a Freedom rider in 1961, was a founding member of SNCC, helped organize the March on Washington, D.C. in 1963, Freedom Summer in '64, the Selma to Montgomery march in '65 where he suffered a fractured skull. Of his many beatings, times in jail and injuries, he said, "We were determined not to let any act of violence keep us from our goal. We knew our lives could be threatened, but we had made up our minds not to turn back."

John Lewis, Dr. Martin Luther King, Jr, Fannie Lou Hamer and many other courageous African American Civil Rights leaders were my models for standing up to the Vietnam war, being willing to sacrifice my life if necessary to contribute to the cause of peace, justice and racial equality.

If these leaders and Thich Nhat Hanh could respond with love and compassion to violence and hatred, I could withstand the vitriol thrown toward me for the Dow action and other times I stand up against racism today.

I particularly appreciated Lewis's ability to extend the message of nonviolent action to young people in his amazing graphic autobiography *March*.

Kamala Harris

August 12, 2020

I'm happy Kamala Harris is Joe Biden's choice as running mate! FINALLY, a decision! Many great women's names were considered, dissected in the press. But there was a strong push for Biden to choose a woman of color, especially after George Floyd's murder in May, 2020. White supremacy doesn't yield easily and won't in the voting process either. Biden did the right thing in choosing a strong woman with national name recognition who wants the job of president. It was an example of a white male, clearly in the position of white supremacy, making an antiracist/feminist choice. Now she is the first African American, South Asian and first woman in US history to become vice-president!

In her initial run for the Democratic nomination, Harris recalled the timing and colors of the campaign literature of Shirley Chisholm. She was the first Black woman to run for President in 1972, another outspoken fighter for the rights of women and African American people.

In her various campaigns, Chisholm said she received greater opposition as a woman (including from some Black men) than she did as a Black woman. She called for a bloodless revolution, and in her presidential announcement said, "I am not the candidate of Black America, although I am black and proud. I am not the candidate of the women's movement of this country, although I am a woman and equally proud of that. I am the candidate of the people and my presence before you symbolizes a new era in American political history."

It would be a racist view that Kamala Harris will have no power as US vice-president! Biden's decision and their win may not constitute revolution, but it is a decision that speaks to the rights of women and Black people for equality in this country.

And he did not come to his decision as an individual. The massive protests demanding a shift in power were the real pressure behind the decision. Power does not concede power easily.

HOPE - Michelle Obama

August 19, 2020

Listening to Michelle Obama's speech at the Democratic Convention, I felt a surge of hope again, hope for an end to the horrible killings of Black people this spring and fall (and many years before), hope for an end to the deadly armed attacks - those supporting white supremacy in this country led by the out-going president. The world needs HOPE.

"Going HIGH!"

Much of what Michelle Obama said in her speech was exactly what I needed to hear at this point in my story about waking up to racism, what people in this country need to hear now.

"Don't give up!"

"Things can and will get worse…so, vote as if your life depended on it! It does!"

"When you see something that's not right, you must DO something."

She said that people have asked her "When others are going so low, does going high still really work?"

"My answer: going high is the only thing that works, because when we go low, when we use those same tactics of degrading and dehumanizing others, we become part of the ugly noise that's drowning out everything else," she said. "We degrade ourselves. We degrade the very causes for which we fight."

"Show up with passion and hope - compassion, resilience!"

"Stand fierce against hatred and find a way to LIVE Together!"

Today I aim for her empathy, her courage, her consistent message of hope for All Americans, for the world, but I have a long way to go in "taking the high road."

Giving up, believing the lies, letting in the voices that would defeat us, giving in to anger, retaliation, despair is just not an option. Not if we want to live. To live, we must build a world where everyone can live free, where we can listen and speak with true empathy and understanding. It is a daily choice to do so.

Every morning, I need to journal, meditate, exercise, write, listen, grow. I need to take care of this precious flame of hope, to remain on the higher road of hope, compassion and trust in a future where every individual's life is valued.

Barack Obama

August 21, 2020

We owe it to our ancestors to VOTE!

I listened to President Obama's speech at the Democratic Convention also. I'll never forget that I lived to see the first Black President in US history elected. He had real Black Power and still does. On the other hand, even an African American president couldn't transform racism completely in this country in eight years. No one could. We have a long way to go, one day, one year, one vote at a time. Perhaps some of us forgot, became complacent during those eight years, left too much up to Obama. We weren't prepared for the backlash (Coates, 2017).

His criticism of the present administration was clear and explicit - that the consequences have included over 430,000 Americans dead of the coronavirus, jobs gone, democratic institutions eroded, the economy - especially for the poor - bottoming, the planet's survival threatened.

He summoned the image of John Lewis walking into jail protesting an end to racist policies on the day Obama was born.

He reminded us that we are grandchildren of ancestors who were beaten, jailed, even killed so we would have the right to vote. Didn't they suffer the same disappointments in the slowness of change, the same despair at racists being elected, the same daily grind of poverty, unemployment, unjust laws and policies? The temptation of cynicism? Yet they fought, they marched, leaders like Martin Luther King and John Lewis and Rosa Parks kept shouting, leading, demanding that the Constitution of the US be "brought to life."

In my heart, I gave up decades ago on this democratic system alone having the power to bring about the changes I'd like to see in this country - true racial and sexual equality, justice, freedom, a beloved community. I didn't bother to vote in a couple of elections because I saw myself as trying to overthrow the entire capitalist system.

Before the last election, I heard someone who saw herself as a radical leftist saying, "Bring on the chaos. We have to destroy everything in order to build a new world order. It doesn't matter who is elected. They're all the same!" Perhaps I saw my old self in her. But, especially living with a Black man for five years, I realized that it does make a difference who is in power. It makes a difference to those who have marginal jobs, who suffer from police brutality or lack of food and medical care. I could no longer take positions that brought such great damage to real people's lives, mostly to Black lives.

I vote now, fortunately because my felonies were reduced to one misdemeanor on appeal, and will continue to vote for these reasons:

- I owe it to those who died to protect the right to vote.
- The alternative is what we have now - far greater suffering for Black, Brown, Indigenous people of color, the poor, women, immigrants, those who already suffer. They are always the ones to suffer first and suffer the most. They are the ones dying of Covid at the highest rates.
- The harm done to others and to our planet is so great that any effort to stop it is an effort to save our own lives, now and for future generations.

Whatever our visions of the future, if we want to have a future, we must halt the present disaster.

LET THE GRANDCHILDREN SPEAK!!!

2020

Protest in Washington, DC over police murders 2020. By Rick Reinhard

Most of the rest of what I have to say about war/peace, suffering/joy, violence/non-violence, racism/antiracism, sexism/feminism, activism/rest will be said through the voices of younger people. I have learned a great deal from young people of color and gratefully pass on the challenge I was given to them. Live a life of speaking out, listening, looking deeply at suffering. Do everything possible, with each precious moment of life, to create peace, beauty, compassion and love for ourselves and our world.

One of the young, aware women to whom I listen carefully is my college-age granddaughter. She was very busy during this pandemic, sequestering with her parents and her film collective, working on university publications, finishing classwork and creating new film projects. She took the time to give me an in depth answer to my questions to her about antiracist work. I will quote just a few of the responses from her on-line exchanges with other students here:

WHERE TO DONATE

Justice for Breonna Taylor

Black Visions Collective in MN

The Audre Lorde Project

TGI Justice

National Black Food & Justice Alliance

Equal Justice Initiative

I donated my entire 'dole' of $1200 from the government to some of the groups above, in addition to local Meals on Wheels, Casa de Maryland, the NAACP, SPLC, ACLU, the Hope Project, Foundation for Suicide Prevention, recovery programs and the Thich Nhat Hanh Foundation. I also decided to donate profits from this book to organizations that support antiracist work.

WHAT TO READ

Whiteness as Property - Cheryl Harris

On Intersectionality: Essential Writings - Kimberlé Crenshaw

Why I'm No Longer Talking to White People About Race - Reni Eddo-Lodge

The Fire Next Time - James Baldwin

Is Prison Necessary? - Ruth Wilson Gilmore

The New Jim Crow - Michelle Alexander

Sister Outsider - Audre Lorde

Are Prisons Obsolete? - Angela Davis

How to be an Antiracist - Ibram X. Kendi

I finished five of these works this summer, in addition to *Just Mercy* by Bryan Stevenson, *Subtle Acts of Exclusion* by Tiffany Jana and Michael Baran, *Girl, Woman, Other* by Bernardine Evaristo, Langston Hughes' Selected Poems, *My Grandmother's Hands* by Resmaa Menakem and *Stamped from the Beginning* by Ibram X. Kendi. Our local Takoma Park Mobilization education group read and discussed *The Color of Law* by Richard Rothstein. Now I'm working to include notes here from *Caste* by Isabel Wilkerson.

WHAT TO WATCH

13th (an excellent look at the history of prisons in the US)

When They See Us (unjust prosecution and imprisonment)

Pose (a glimpse into transgender life during the AIDS epidemic)

Just Mercy - (read the book too)

1965 Debate between James Baldwin and William F. Buckley

I Am Not Your Negro

Fruitvale Station

I would add *Moonlight, If Beale St. Could Talk, Black KKlansman, Get Out, Dear White People, Harriet, The Black Panther, Ma Rainey's Black Bottom* and *Kaun*.

IDEAS TO CONSIDER

- Productive White Allyship
- Educate yourself: You cannot expect a person of color to educate you; you need to do it yourself.
- Speak up, but don't speak over : You have a duty to speak out for the victims of institutional racism, but you do not have any right to speak over them.
- Do not expect praise.
- Start conversations with other white people: This is a very concrete role you, as a white person, can have. Take your newfound knowledge from educating yourself and put it into practice by talking to your friends and starting difficult conversations! Many people will never put themselves into situations where these discussions happen, so you can have a role in making them happen. If you get the ball rolling with your friends, family, and acquaintances, you can really make a difference.
- Stand up for the movement even when it's uncomfortable: This goes along with the last point. Did your significant other just make a racist joke? Are your family members making uninformed statements about a recent court case at the dinner table? If you remain silent, you're contributing to a society that normalizes racism.
- Make becoming an ally part of your daily life: It is within your privilege as a white person to have the ability to choose when you want to protest. People of color do not

have the same lack of urgency; racial inequality directly and negatively impacts their lives every day.
- Reflect on your or others' use of microaggressions: Microaggressions are the everyday verbal, nonverbal, and environmental slights, snubs, or insults, whether intentional or unintentional, that communicate hostile, derogatory, or negative messages to target persons based solely upon their marginalized group membership. Some examples are:
- A person asking an Asian American or Latino American to teach them words in their native language.
- Not listening closely and learning the pronunciation of a non-English based names. Continuing to mispronounce the names of people after they have corrected the person time and time again.
- "I'm not racist. I have several Black friends." "As a woman, I know what you go through as a racial minority."
- "When I look at you, I don't see color."
- Understand that you too are a racial subject: White people often have the privilege of distancing themselves from race. It is a privilege to have a "colorblind" attitude, which dismisses and invalidates the lived experiences of people of color. Acknowledge your blind spots and implicit biases.
- (For examples of applying some of these principles to the

workplace, see *Subtle Acts of Exclusion* by Tiffany Jana and Michael Baran).

Specific Policy Change Suggestions by Young People:

- Redirect finances away from the military and police to healthcare, employment, affordable housing, education and anti-violence solutions.
- Rather than 'reform' measures for police policies, some groups are calling for defunding and abolishing police departments as inherently racist institutions. One quote from the Instagram debate makes a powerful argument:

The case against police reform:

"It is impossible to reform a police state. The system is not broken, it was designed to oppress and it has been doing that perfectly. The police, since their inception, have always upheld white supremacy as an institution. There is an uninterrupted continuum of anti-Black violence throughout the history of the American police force. The right offers more policing as a solution to the problem of police violence. Firing or arresting the few bad cops has not and will not do anything because the institution of policing is inherently violent. Superficial solutions are not enough.

Remove police from schools, repeal laws criminalizing survival, free people from prisons and jails, care for drug addicts and the mentally ill rather than killing them. Call a Granny, not a cop for domestic cases!

Question the capitalist view that education, healthcare and basic survival needs should be for-profit. WHY? Doesn't every human being deserve to have basic human needs met?"

— Unknown, appears to be collective thoughts.

Young people's voices are powerful! Inspiring! Motivating us elders to LISTEN! CONNECT to others to keep learning and ACT to build community and a more just society. There are basic human rights that everyone in a democratic society should have. Don't children have a human right to eat, to be clothed, sheltered, cared for, educated? Is this socialism or just common sense?

The passion and sometimes absolutism in the goals of some movement groups today definitely remind me of many of our demands in the '60s and '70's for an end to capitalist exploitation of the working class, an end to the military, nuclear weapons, chemical weapons, war, poverty, racism and sexism. I must say that age and experience have mellowed my most extreme views and amplified the need for non-violence in our actions. I see that the extremes of Left and Right are more alike than different.

We need goals, visions of possible communities and countries where the welfare of people is more important than profit. Where non-violence, peace-making and compassion is taught to young children rather than war games. There are examples, models, such as Bhutan, which measures the "Gross National Happiness" of the country as a constitutional goal! Without such visions of a nonviolent community, of equality, generosity and love, a future is not possible for us.

Kaun កូន

2020

In addition to her powerful words, here is my granddaughter Annelise's amazing short film - Kaun ("Child" in Khmai). She just published it September 16, 2020. It's AWESOME! Truly! It begins with the voice of her Cambodian grandmother grieving over the loss of her two-year old baby during the Khmer Rouge genocide. Then we hear Annelise's voice speaking as her grandmother to her only surviving family member from the Khmer Rouge, her eldest child. She gives her freedom and hope as they begin a new life in America...but with the echoes of all the voices, faces, lives of those they saw die in Cambodia.

Annelise's description:

"This short film imagines the voice of my grandmother speaking to my mother as they arrive in the United States after escaping the genocide in Cambodia. The project engages with family, memory, erasure, and resilience in the absence of a personal archive."

The poetry coming from my granddaughter is art I will never achieve, talent that goes way beyond mine. Isn't this always the wish of every mother - that their children and grandchildren will achieve skills, life and happiness beyond our own? I'm proud of her, so happy that she cares enough to voice her mother, grandmother, all those children's voices shut off from speaking of their suffering and dreams. She embodies her heritage, gives images and poetry the world needs so much now.

Let me be quiet! It speaks for itself! Listen.

You can find this film on YouTube: **Kaun**

Her website www.anneliseratner.com has more of her short films, including *All the Difference* about our DC-9 action.

HOW TO BUILD BELOVED COMMUNITIES

"Once the hate is gone, they will be forced to be with the pain."

— James Baldwin

In addition to reading Kendi, Menakem, Davis, Stevenson, Wilkerson, Coates and many other wonderful African American authors this summer, listening to the political debates and the wisdom of the young, I also attended seminars and retreats where teachers directly addressed the police killings, the effects of the coronavirus and gave us suggestions about how to transform this suffering in ourselves and in the world.

Fortunately, many of the voices of these teachers in my community are powerful people of color who are members of the Order of Interbeing, ordained to teach by Thich Nhat Hanh.

When I was six years sober, I had for those years been guided by my sponsor, and other friends in the recovery program to develop a strong practice of morning meditation to stay sober. But I felt I needed more help with meditation, so I agreed to join my son in a retreat with Thich Nhat Hanh. In preparation for the retreat, I read *The Miracle of Mindfulness* by this Vietnamese Buddhist teacher. The Introduction described my first experience hearing him speak in 1968! The same man exiled from his country for speaking out for peace and who had instituted Engaged Buddhism, an activist I admired! He had been the same monk who had so touched my heart and helped me decide to do the DC-9 action!

The retreat was wonderful. I had found my new spiritual home! After many more retreats with this community over the years, my husband and I were ordained by him into the OI in 2011.

The Order of Inter-being was formed by Thich Nhat Hanh in 1966 amidst the war in Vietnam, to bring together young people helping refugees and orphans from the bombings to support one another. During the pandemic, members of the OI from around the world gathered on line to sustain one another and explore what to do about all the deaths, illness and police killings going on.

Below are some of the words of OI speakers at this summer's zoom retreats, which guide us in building strong communities of peace, love and understanding to make a future for our human race possible.

KAIRA JEWEL LINGO

"Juneteenth" June 19, 2020

I participated in a powerful ninety minute workshop Honoring Juneteenth, the announcement of the end of slavery in Galveston, TX on June 19, 1865 that "all slaves are FREE."

Kaira Jewel Lingo, a beautiful African American dharma teacher (who was a nun in Thich Nhat Hanh's community for fifteen years) led us in a guided meditation in which she recited George Floyd's words in the last six minutes of his life:

> "Please, please, I can't breathe
> Please, man, somebody
> Please, man, I can't breathe…
> I can't move..
> Mama, Mama, I can't..
> My knee…My neck…I'm through…I'm
>   through..
> My stomach hurts…My neck hurts.
> Everything hurts.
> Please, I can't breathe, officer.
> They're gonna kill me.
> I cannot breathe…
> Please sir, please…
> Please…
> I can't breathe."

— Lingo, 2020

We breathed in and out, hearing these words in her gentle voice, the pauses in between the words, feeling the impact of those nine minutes in our bodies, tears flowing.

It was a very painful but transformative experience, so I decided I would repeat this meditation for a local group of people who were suffering fear, anger, rage, impotence in the face of Floyd's murder. They needed, as I did, to feel the horror of that slow, deliberate squeezing out of a human life, to feel the impact of racism in our bodies and minds. But they also needed to calm the rage, the fear, to find enough calm from which to discern what to do about the injustice. We kept breathing, nourishing life, peace and connection with one another to lessen the pain of loss, anger and loneliness. This first guided meditation experience has continued every week during our ten-month Covid retreat and is expected to continue on line as long as needed.

Then, Kaira Jewel, talked about the generations of African American people, including her own family, who have suffered the long-term effects of slavery, injustice and inequality in our country. To transform racist policies and institutions, we must understand not only the victims of racism but the perpetrators who killed George Floyd. This cruelty toward Black people has been inherited by white people who descend from immigrants tortured, pilloried and imprisoned for minor crimes. They continue to pass on their inherited suffering to others. She said that to transform this suffering in both Black and white bodies and minds, we need to understand our history, see both the suffering and the resilience of our ancestors and work to transform our trauma and undo the system of white supremacy in our country.

In the workshop, we listened to horrible descriptions of slavery, saw pictures of lynchings, heard the voices of slaves and their sharecropper children testifying to the cruelty of whippings, killings, children torn from mothers' arms to be sold in far-away states. We meditated on the trauma of slavery and oppression alive in our own bodies, Black and white bodies, transmitted by our ancestors, experienced ourselves in the 21st century.

We discussed how slavery continued for years in share-cropping and Jim Crow laws, lynchings, the false imprisonments, economic, social and political enslavement of African Americans that continues to this day in every institution in our society. Racism lives, of course, in our minds and hearts; but more importantly it is the institutionalized POWER of white supremacy that keeps crushing African Americans under its knee.

After the workshop, my husband and I continued to honor Juneteenth by driving along 16th St.NW, the route to the White House with the thousands lined up on porches, marching in streets throughout D.C.. We displayed posters in the windows of the car - "Pardon the inconvenience while we CHANGE our WORLD," and "BE the change you want to see in the world" and, of course, "BLACK LIVES MATTER!"

In the evening we listened to Sweet Honey in the Rock sing powerful Civil Rights songs, chant dozens of names of Black people killed in the last two years and keen the sorrow of their mothers and grandmothers.

The music and poetry that has arisen from slavery continues to uplift and inspire us today:

From "Freedom's Plow":

> "Who is America? You, me!
> We are America!
> To the enemy who would conquer us from without,
> We say, NO!
> To the enemy who would divide
> And conquer us from within,
> We say NO!
> FREEDOM!
> BROTHERHOOD!
> DEMOCRACY!
> ….Keep your hand on the plow! HOLD ON!"
>
> — HUGHES, 1959

VALERIE BROWN

For the June Day of Mindfulness, our main speaker on zoom was Valerie Brown, another African American dharma teacher in the tradition of Thich Nhat Hanh. She is a member of Arise, an international mindfulness group dedicated to awakening through race, intersectionality, and social equity. They come together to heal the wounds of racial injustice and social inequity, beginning with looking deeply within ourselves and using the energy of compassion, understanding and love in action.

She said that we were in a perfect storm of pandemic affecting people of color in much higher proportions that the general population, along with the many killings of Black people by police. She reminded us that we are not alone in facing these crises, that wise teachers have given us a model of fighting injustice without hate. Our fates are interdependent with those causing our suffering. She encouraged us to follow the example of John Lewis and continue to make "good trouble" (Brown,2020).

SISTER PEACE

During our July Day of Mindfulness on line for members of the Order of Interbeing, Sister Peace, an African American member of our own Washington Mindfulness Community, now an ordained nun and dharma teacher, spoke. She reminded us that July 26 would have been Emmett Till's 79th birthday had he not been killed at age 14 for whistling at a white woman in Mississippi.

Sister Peace works at a juvenile detention center in Memphis, teaching sitting and hugging meditation to young African American men. She teaches them about the 400 years of slavery, Jim Crow and an unjust criminal justice system that led them to be where they are now. She also let them know that it was there in Nashville that Martin Luther King led sanitation workers to strike with signs saying "I am a Man." The spirit was similar to the Black Live Matters movement of today. Our humanity has been under assault and we need to stand up, protest, speak out our truth.

She urged us to have the courage to share openly in our communities, to talk about the composition of our groups, share openly about racism and its effects on all of us, explore uncomfortable feelings and create safe spaces together. We celebrate our differences and the common unity that binds us all (Sr Peace/Plum Village, 2020).

LARRY WARD

"We must transform racism into equality to survive!"

— Larry Ward

Larry Ward is another African American meditation teacher, founder of the Lotus Institute based in Atlanta. The assassination of Dr. Martin Luther King, Jr., changed Larry's life. He was searching for direction when this killing called him into community service, spiritual growth and planetary peacemaking. He and Kaira Jewel Lingo, both African American teachers ordained by Thich Nhat Hanh, presented another powerful webinar I attended.

Some of the highlights of Larry's talk:

"We live in the matrix, this age of electronics where technology guides us to what we already know and believe, reinforces those beliefs.

I trust in our human spirit that cannot be contained only in form. The spirit is bigger than this body, these structures and cultures we live in. We need a sangha, a community, in order to be together, to know who we are....to go beyond the limits of one. We need small groups, pods, groups where we can hold our sanity.

It may take years to transform our white supremacy. Racism is not at the level of the mind only...it's in our bodies, in trauma that we have carried now for over 400 years.

What's at stake is our own human sovereignty, working on our emotions, resisting the urge to freeze, to be immobilized... If we do not transform these habits into true equality...

We will NOT SURVIVE!

I feel safe in nature. Nature is not out there!

WE ARE NATURE!

Dualism is the tragedy of our lives. Seeing ourselves as separate from nature, others, our own bodies, our history. We are here because of the sorrow, joy and energy of our ancestors and nature. Go into your roots! Don't abandon them!

Icebergs are melting and who's talking about it? We have to be enhanced… til we're big enough to comprehend that we are part of this vast Universe. The Universe IS us! Our neurons need to be re-wired. Neuro-plasticity is what humans ARE.

"Anima Mundi" - We need a new world soul; we need feelings, values that transcend structures. Go into your dream space and see what's there. Connection! Vibration! Imagination!

We know it's possible to transform because we wouldn't be here otherwise…for this new form of "slouching toward Bethlehem."

> The reference to Yeats' poem,
> "The Second Coming":
> "The darkness drops again; but now I know
> That twenty centuries of stony sleep
> Were vexed to nightmare by a rocking
>   cradle,
> And what rough beast, its hour come round
>   at last,
> Slouches towards Bethlehem to be born?"

The main thing We Have To Do is process our unprocessed trauma. My own personal trauma is linked to UNIVERSAL trauma. I saw how deeply transmitted pain could be. What a deep spiritual practice it is to look deeply into our own minds and hearts, to recall the suffering of our ancestors. We can't think ourselves out of trauma, we have to do the work, dig deeply into our unconsciousness, into our bodies.

We need to deepen meditation into contemplation…so we can escape the Matrix. How conscious are we willing to be? We have to distinguish between what we're doing, saying…have to ask - WHAT DO WE WANT, what are our values? What are we willing to DO?

Some things we humans create are downright evil. Why? Because we are not fully aware of what we are doing? Creating? We have to learn to BE where we ARE, when we walk, just walk. When we cook, just cook. Our actions matter, they last into the future. It is only by learning to be deeply in the present moment that we take actions to change our future for the better.

We don't have to hide….there is brutality…and we are either witnesses, perps or victims. Did you watch the video of George Floyd's murder? Am I frozen, not able to FEEL another's pain? Gradually this process of awakening becomes a state of having your heart broken over and over. Are we willing to face this heartbreak, to FEEL the suffering of our ancestors, ourselves and people suffering in our society in order to heal the trauma?

Our dilemma is what we do ….we have to heal ourselves into beauty… need retreats to heal trauma. We have to de-traumatize ourselves and uncover our true nature.

Underneath trauma is GLORY…get a coach, a trainer…we've been working on this for a long time….Black people have Gospel, jazz. We are resilient already! White people need help.

Western medicine only sees pathology, when what we need is prevention, looking at the whole of our nature, not just the negative illness or symptoms. Our ancestors also had resilience, survival instincts, magic, poetry, song.

Hang with people who nourish you. There is enough negativity in the news, enough suffering in the world. We don't need to increase it. But it's important to be with people who encourage your hope, laughter, creativity, sanity.

Use your imagination - put what you want into poetry, dance, song! LIVE!"

For more of Larry Ward's insights see *America's Racial Karma: An Invitation to Heal* and similar thinking in Resmaa Menakem's *Our Grandmother's Hands* (Ward, The Lotus Institute, 2020 & 2021).

My Reflections

These talks energized my spirit, gave me even more motivation for putting this message out to the world.

People need HOPE that we can change, that we can survive the incredible forces leading us and our planet to destruction.

We can't run away from what is really happening! We need to face it, look at the pandemic, not try to run, escape. FACE IT. Face the fact that the polar cap is melting, Greenland's borders are disappearing! The Antarctic is breaking apart. We are facing such huge changes on our planet. Many people are afraid and suffering, especially during this Covid pandemic, at unconscious levels of their beings. We have been suffering from racism for centuries. Are we ready to be part of our new reality, to look it in the face and make clear decisions about what to do?

The harm done to this country by our history of slavery and racism is exploding. We are divided and we cannot afford to be divided in this state of world crises.

Did forty percent of the people in the US vote to cling to a structure and system of white supremacy, of patriarchy, suppressing and killing people of color, women, immigrants?

Are they afraid of losing their identity?

Security?

Is it FEAR?

Are some fearful of the energy and power of "women who roar" and tell the truth about rape?

Fearful of Black people as articulate, creative and visionary as Larry Ward, Spike Lee, Fred Hampton, Toni Morrison, Angela Davis, Kaira Jewel?

Barack Obama must have terrified some racists with his grace, dignity and brilliance. There is no "them" and "us." We are them; they are us. Which aspect of ourselves and our culture do we water today?

We won't shut up. We won't shrink in fear. We will shout, speak out, speak up, keep creating amazing art. We will do the work of looking deeply within ourselves, being courageous enough to face the demons of racism and sexism within ourselves and our culture. We are committed to transforming that history, those crimes against ourselves and against people of color. We have the resources, the history, the heroes and heroines within us. We are powerful…strong…invincible. We are life itself.

Racism is something we can heal. We need to…to survive…we need to STOP, just STOP the fear, the killing, the divisions, the hatred….to hold those people who are so afraid that they are willing to kill strangers because of the color of their skin. To heal them. But first we must STOP the killing.

Racism did not always exist. It had a beginning in the 15th century. Hopefully it will end on the 21st. Other systems have changed, have been destroyed. So can racism be destroyed, overcome, transformed!

I am one human being, a tiny cell in the vast Universe, but I must do what I can, with the time left to me. I will not die. I will live on in those who love me, in my words, my actions. Just as Martin Luther King, Malcolm X, John Lewis, Rosa Parks and Ruth Bader Ginsberg live on in us. Help us, ancestors, all you forces of goodness, love, peace and freedom, to keep writing, keep creating, listening, touching LIFE and moving toward LIFE.

Breathing, helping others stop and BREATHE.

SURVIVE!

LIVE!

TRANSFORM!

Building Harmony in the Community

One theme of this book is "building beloved communities" where harmony, compassion, peace and love reign. I felt those qualities in our diverse neighborhood in October as we celebrated a holiday focused on delighting children and the child in us adults. I have been privileged to live in various forms of community all of my life - with my birth family, my church, neighborhood and school communities, the Loretto community, the women's, antiracist and anti-war movements, communes, my African American family with Jeff, recovery communities, sanghas and life today with my husband, son and his family.

Once a month, I join my worldwide meditation community - the Order of Interbeing - to recite the 14 MindfulnessTrainings.

I need this reminder of my vow to "take a clear stand against oppression and injustice…without taking sides in a conflict." A difficult challenge during national election debates and yet another killing of a young Black man - Kevin E. Peterson, Jr, 21 - by police in Portland.

My challenge is to extend the same understanding, compassion and love to the police and people with opposing political views that I give to beloved brothers and sisters in my Order of Interbeing community.

WHAT DO WE DO TO END RACISM?

The central purpose of *AWAKE to Racism* is to help people see, feel and understand the suffering of Black people in the US and how this traumatic injustice affects all people, harms us all, calls us to stay awake and to act with courage and commitment to end to white supremacy - for a future to be possible for us all.

How would I summarize key lessons in my constant process of waking up to racism?

- OPEN MINDS to the truth and power of Black people's message and experience.

Stay informed, read, study, learn, face the reality, the history & horror of racism.

- Make Black friends, experience suffering and survival, tears and laughter, blues and jazz.
- Allow communities to support us and shine the light on our failings, our racist ideas and actions and be open to healthy criticism and change.
- Realize that we "inter-are"! All our thoughts, words, deeds affect others as they affect us. We are ONE human race, to live or vanish together.
- Act on convictions and develop courage to "do the right thing" with boldness.
- Love guides us, changes us, unites us, and trumps hate.
- A spiritual vision of unity, compassion, and love infuses the most effective, persistent efforts to abolish racism, sexism, homophobia, war, violence. I have to start inside myself, with my own fear, anger, vengeance, judgment, dualistic thinking, but also be willing to take action in the community to change policies, injustice.
- WE ARE ONE, so harming one group of people harms ALL of US! No one is immune. As long as one is oppressed, all of us are oppressed.
- CHANGE is possible, necessary, inevitable, constant.
- A multi-ethnic, multi-colored community is beautiful, happening now, whether we like it or not.

Healing daily from my alcoholism has been a process; so is healing our country from the legacy of slavery and oppression of African American people. In *Caste*, Isabel Wilkerson says,

"Slavery is commmonly dismissed as a 'sad, dark chapter' in the country's history. It is as if the greater the distance we can create between slavery and ourselves, the better to stave off the guilt or shame it induces.

But in the same way that individuals cannot move forward, become whole and healthy, unless they examine the domestic violence they witnessed as children or the alcoholism that runs in their family, the country cannot become whole until it confronts what was not a chapter in its history, but the basis of its economic and social order. For a quarter millennium, slavery *was* the country." (Isabel Wilkerson, 2020,43.)

Do White People BENEFIT from Antiracist Policies?

In the Epilogue to *Stamped from the Beginning* by Ibram X. Kendi, he traces how racist ideas have been articulated since Greek and Roman days, and explains enslavement theories based on Genesis referring to the "Curse of Ham." He explains that racial inferiority was specifically directed at Africans from the days of the Portuguese slave trade in the 15th century. So there was a long history to the link between racist ideas and economic power.

In his conclusion, he reiterates how moral, educational persuasion hasn't worked to eliminate racism. The root problem is not ignorance and hatred, but self-interest. He traces how ineffective and even racist some views of integration, abolition, "uplift suasion," and assimilation have been throughout U.S. history. It is a false notion that racists just don't know the facts of the oppression of people of color. He maintains that "In fact, self-interest leads to racist policies, which lead to racist ideas leading to all the ignorance and hate. Racist policies were created out of self-interest." *(Ibid, 506)* Thus, racist policies have usually been voluntarily rolled back out of self-interest.

How have poor, unemployed, working class white people in the US been persuaded that racial policies against Black people benefit them? That they result in better jobs, health care, homes, education for their children than antiracist policies have done? *History demonstrates the opposite - that white people (except the 1% of white, heterosexual, Protestant, non-immigrant, super rich men) actually benefit from antiracist policies.*

White people don't need to be altruistic, self-sacrificial or deprived of any human rights or even prosperity in order to bring about a truly antiracist society. EVERYONE will benefit and has benefited historically, from policies that ensure equality in courts of law, education, jobs, healthcare and more equitable distribution of wealth and resources.

Kendi emphasizes throughout his writing that to be antiracist, views and policies must also be free of sexism, homophobia, xenophobia and any form of discrimination or inequality toward any group of people. None of us truly benefit or gain real privilege from any form of oppression. The opposite is true - that the more we insist on the value and equality of every human being, the more we all benefit.

He concludes that when antiracists are in power antiracist policies will become the "common sense" of a truly equitable society. "When we fight for humanity, we are fighting for ourselves." Everyone benefits!

Then our entire country will become a beloved community. In order to reach that goal, we begin building equitable communities where we are - in our homes, neighborhoods, schools, workplaces, churches and social groups where we live now. We organize and demand equality in all institutions, extending it to those who have long suffered without it. It is in our interest to do so. In fact, our society and our world cannot survive without equality.

How Can We Survive Beautifully into the Future?

My gratitude for the great privilege of being a mother and grandmother fills my heart. My son and granddaughter are my physical, biological, tangible continuation into the future. But like those who do not have children or grandchildren, I have many other forms of my life that will continue beyond this lifetime. Like all other human beings, I will experience ill health, old age and death; but my actions are the ground of my being, the only real inheritance I offer to future generations. Some actions during the years of excessive drinking I regret and have tried to amend. But I have never regretted my five federal felonies or any other actions, legal or illegal, committed in the effort to bring more peace and equality to our troubled world.

Angela Davis and Nicki Giovanni, my contemporaries, are my role models for women of color who persist in their life-long work to transform racism and injustice into equality, justice and beauty:

> "So, even though I know the world always appears to be so chaotic, and sometimes we can't see a way out, I think the work that we have to do is to guarantee that we pass down a legacy to the next group, the next generation. And that's our only hope for achieving change...Many people are under the impression that youth is an eternal. It doesn't happen that way. Before you know it, you will have aged out of youth...It's so important to train others to share. And with each generation, it becomes richer and more interesting and more complicated... as I get older, I realize how important it is for us to imagine ourselves as something more than our own individual lives, that we're connected with people who came before us, and we will be connected to people who come after us. So, it's our responsibility ... and the responsibility of younger people, too, to make sure that you do the work that will keep the ideas alive, that will keep the possibility of freedom alive."

— From 1968 to 2018: Angela Davis on Freedom Struggles Then and Now, and the Movements of the Future, 12/24/18 Part 3

AND FURTHER INSPIRING words from Nikki Giovanni:

> "I thought fifty years ago that I could make a big difference in the world. What I know now is that I will not allow the world to make a big difference in me. That's what's incredibly important. I'm not going to let the fact that I live in a nation with a bunch of fools make a fool out of me."
>
> "I am an old lady, which I recommend," she said. "I really like what the young people are doing, and I think my job is to be sure to get out of their way, but also let them know, if it means anything to them, that I'm proud of them… "I recommend old age," she said. "There's just nothing as wonderful as knowing you have done your job."
>
> — NIKKI GIOVANNI, FINDING THE SONG IN THE DARKEST DAYS BY ELIZABETH A. HARRIS, 12/16/20

I thank you readers who have traveled with me on this journey of reflection and attempt to honor the voices of People of Color whose lives were taken unjustly and of those who fight against the injustice of white supremacy. If an ignorant white kid from the midwest who grew up in a totally segregated system can change, can wake up to the horrors of racism and participate in the on-going struggle against it, anyone can. Our waking up is a process that will hopefully last for the rest of our lives. We continue to listen, connect with our neighbors, co-workers, teachers, leaders, our families and build the beloved communities that Dr. Martin Luther King Jr spoke of in 1963 in his "I Have a Dream" speech.

"I have a dream... that one day on the red hills of Georgia, the sons of former slaves and the sons of former slave owners will be able to sit down together at the table of brotherhood."

We are building those communities now. Wise, resilient, generous, loving people have been doing so for centuries. We follow in their footsteps, making mistakes, but moving forward, opening our hearts more widely to include those who are sickened by fear and hatred.

"We are the ones we have been waiting for"

We are the ones we have been waiting for, Alice Walker says in her 2006 book, because we live in an age in which we are able to see and understand our own predicament. With so much greater awareness than our ancestors – and with such capacity for insight, knowledge, and empathy –we are uniquely prepared to create positive change within ourselves and our world.

Yet our efforts are imperfect. These are reflections on my experiences at this moment in time. NOT a definitive anything, just a speck of writing from one person's perspective and experience. An older white woman who wants to be an effective antiracist, to stand up in any way possible with my African American friends against injustice. I want to speak out for true equality, fairness, unity for *all people*, especially people of color who have been enslaved, suffered discrimination, deprivation and murder because of their skin color.

As a human, I am by nature imperfect. I make mistakes. I have much left to learn. Like all humans, I am of the nature to become ill, to grow old, to be separated from those I love, to die. All humans suffer, but we also have the capacity to learn the causes of our suffering and to find a path to transform suffering into peace. We are able to listen to the suffering of others, to understand and empathize, to do our best to love one another and be part of the solution to social ills that cause suffering to so many.

I was asked in an interview recently, "What gives you hope?"

My first answer was - "My granddaughter!" Her resilience, creativity, courage, her ability to be silent, listening to suffering, then to transform that suffering into art. Her skill, honed, practiced, gained through trial, error and persistence results in beautiful films. She amazes me. Her generation inspires me. I trust young people to carry on the best of our work to make this world a better place.

What else gives me hope? - the sun rising, the full moon, the waves continuing to lap the shores all over the world, the stars, the galaxies. Babies give me hope. Science gives me hope. Old folks walking, doing Qi Gong, learning new languages and skills, singing their songs. Human beings give me hope. Recovering alcoholics and addicts. My niece who survived breast cancer and now Covid 19 and still teaches music to her students online. The constant loveof my husband gives me hope. My son and daughter-in-love inspire me with their world-shaking work and art. Every morning I wake up alive, I have hope that racism can end, that human beings can learn to live as one. One day at a time, one moment at a time, life persists in our breath, in our love for one another.

Daily, I witness miracles of transformation. I have a photo on my wall of a Black man hugging the white woman who killed his brother, thinking he was breaking into her apartment. She had opened the wrong door in the apartment, shot the man who lived there, was convicted of murder. The brother forgave her.

Among my friends, I regularly see people transform from lives of despair and daily drinking to useful, happy, productive lives.

I believe that my relatives who voted for the man who is most responsible today for hundreds of thousands of Black bodies suffering at a rate much higher than white bodies from Covid can change their minds, amend their actions. Even those who invaded the U.S.Capitol resulting in six deaths on January 6, 2021 are capable of change.

I'm writing to wake up other people, as I keep being wakened every day now by both the extremes of hatred and fear I see in acts of racial hatred and the depth of love and compassion I see in people, groups and institutions that have changed. They are not polar opposites. I know both extremes can exist in me. If I can change, keep changing, I believe that every human being has the capacity for transformation, for open-mindedness, empathy, kindness, love. If people can change, governments and policies can be changed.

We sometimes divide ourselves into categories of "Left" and "Right," rigidly defining ourselves into violent confrontation. We have a left hand and a right hand, both part of us, both our body, not separate entities. When the right hand strikes the left hand with a hammer inadvertently, doesn't it drop the hammer and hold that left hand, recognizing that one body is suffering, in need of comfort and healing?

I have to keep reaching for these qualities in my own soul - my extremes of ego, pride, individuality and separateness on the one side and unity, empathy, connection and "inter-being" on the other. Two sides of one coin, two aspects of one body.

God, Universe, help us stop the oppression and killing of Black, Indigenous and People of Color, who represent the majority of people in our country and WORLD!!! Bless all of us with love and much compassion today!

We are in the nexus between past and future. It's time for the Grannies to entrust the future to our next generation. So here are some memories of past efforts to end racism in the last few decades. I hope this book is useful to you and other antiracists. Please write, sing, speak, film, share your story for the generations to come.. Each one of us holds all past generations and all future generations in this body, this mind, this moment. Our actions count. They have the power to ripple outward to others in this moment in time, and to contribute to others in the future. We are all connected. We are waves on one ocean, leaves on one tree, stars in one sky.

We don't know the *full* impact of our words, our actions, our relationships. We just keep doing the next right thing in front of us, the next loving, courageous, antiracist action, taking into consideration that it might have a long-term impact on the earth, the climate, reducing racism, increasing compassion and peace in the Universe in whatever small way. A rock tossed into a lake creates ripples, outward, far from our sight.

"When the student is ready, the teacher will appear" has been my experience all my life, I realize now as I look back and remember both the suffering and serendipitous experiences, I am deeply grateful for my teachers. I am grateful to still be unpeeling the layers of the onion of growth inside me to find the truth of Interbeing, the interconnection and interdependence of all human beings. As I was awakening to the realities of racism in Montgomery, Alabama in 1963, Thich Nhat Hanh was organizing resistance to the racist, imperialist bombing of his country by the US. He was exiled in 1966 for his work of creating a School of Social work with thousands of young people caring for refugees, victims of US bombs and napalm. I was fortunate to meet him in 1968 when his words and actions inspired me to join the DC-9 action against Dow Chemical. Then after years of my own suffering, he reappeared in my life in 1991 and became my meditation teacher.

Our lives, the lives of the people of our two nations and all people of color who have suffered from discrimination are intertwined so deeply, that we must build a new world together to survive. In 2005, I was privileged to travel to Vietnam with him on his first return from exile in thirty-nine years, and see thousands come to hear him and walk with him. I am profoundly grateful that my spiritual teacher is a person of color, one of the wisest, most compassionate teachers on the planet today.

In our meditation group, we are reading and discussing Thich Nhat Hanh's *At Home in the World*:

"I thought about all the children in Vietnam, Cambodia, Somalia, Yugoslavia, and South America, and other places where there is so much suffering, and I felt a strong sense of solidarity with all of them. I felt ready to undergo these hardships with them, again and again.

You, my brothers and sisters, are my companions. You are truly riding on the waves of birth and death, without drowning in birth and death. We have gone though interminable suffering, endless tunnels of sorrow and darkness. But we have practiced, and through the practice, we have obtained some insight and freedom. Now it is time for us to join together and bring our strength to bear on the challenges that lie before us. I am sure we will do better this time (Thich N. Hanh, 2016, 31)."

In a talk in January 2021, after the attack on the Capitol, Larry Ward reminded us that man is not the enemy, that we have enough resources to change this deadly system that is killing all of us. We need courage, unity, compassion, the insight of teachers like Thich Nhat Hanh, who wrote this poem after he heard that four of his young students has been executed in Vietnam in 1965: (Thich N. Hanh, 1993,18).

Recommendation

>Promise me
>promise me this day,
>promise me now,
>while the sun is overhead
>exactly at the zenith,
>promise me:
>
>Even as they
>strike you down
>with a mountain of hatred and violence;
>even as they step on you and crush you
>like a worm,
>even as they dismember and disembowel
>>you,
>
>remember, brother,
>remember:
>man is not our enemy.

The only thing worthy of you is
    compassion -
invincible, limitless, unconditional.
Hatred will never let you face
the beast in man.

One day, when you face this beast alone,
with your courage intact, your eyes kind,
untroubled
(even as no one sees them),
out of your smile
will bloom a flower.
And those who love you
will behold you
across ten thousand worlds of birth and
    dying.

Alone again,
I will go on with bent head,
knowing that love has become eternal.
on the long, rough road,
the sun and the moon
will continue to shine.

— Thich N. Hanh

If I fall asleep, close my eyes and ears to cries for justice, something in my soul begins to die. If I have the courage, transmitted to me by countless ancestors and teachers, to stay awake, a new world awaits my open eyes.

I can breathe.

WE can breathe!

THE END

Say Their Names

Patrick Warren

Quawan Charles

Dijon Kizzee

Julian Lewis

Priscilla Slater

Jamel Floyd

Calvin Horton, Jr.

George Floyd

Steven Taylor

Barry Gedeus

Lionel Morris

Darius Tarver

John Neville

Byron Williams

Dominique Clayton

Sterling Higgins

Aleah Jenkins

Charles Roundtree, Jr.

JasonWashington

Earl McNeil

Danny Ray Thomas

DamonGrimes

Mikel McIntyre

Alteria Woods

Deborah Danner

Christian Taylor

Joseph Mann

Jay Anderson, Jr.

Bettie Jones

Samuel Dubose

Susie Jackson

Myra Thompson

Sharonda Coleman-Singleton

Kalief Browder

Walter Scott

Rumain Brisbon

Tanisha Anderson

Darrien Hunt

Michelle Cusseaux

Amir Brooks

Jerry Dwight Brown

Yvette Smith

Renisha McBride

Gabriel Winzer

Kayla Moore

Corey Stingley

Mohamed Bah

Rekia Boyd

Willie Ray Banks

Robert Ricks

EugeneEllison

Lawrence Allen

Marvin Parker

Kathryn Johnston

Anthony Dwain Lee

James Byrd, Jr.

Sharon Walker

Elton Hayes

Alberta Odell Jones

John Earl Reese

Della McDuffie

Dr. Andrew C. Jackson

Malcolm Wright

Emmett Till

Medgar Evers

Jimmie Lee Jackson

Fred Hampton

Eleanor Bumpurs

Nicholas Heyward Jr.

Ricky Byrdsong

Timothy Stansbury, Jr.

Deaunta Farrow

Oscar Grant

Danroy "DJ" Henry, Jr.

Kenneth Chamberlain, Sr.

Trayvon Martin

Sgt. James Brown

Darnesha Harris

Wayne A. Jones

Jonathan Ferrell

Victor White III

John Crawford III

Dante Parker

Michael Brown

Laquan McDonald

Tamir Rice

Natasha McKenna

Freddie Gray

Clementa Pinckney

Cynthia Hurd

Daniel Simmons

Darrius Stewart

Quintonio Legrier

David Joseph

Philando Castile

Jamarion Robinson

Alfred Olango

Desmond Phillips

Jordan Edwards

James Lacy

Stephon Clark

Marcus-David Peters

Antwon Rose, Jr.

Botham Jean

Emantic Bradford, Jr

Bradley Blackshire

Pamela Turner

Elijah McClain

Michael Dean

Miciah Lee

Jaquyn O'Neill Light

Manuel Ellis

Daniel Prude

Marice Gordon

Tony McDade

David McAtee

Robert Forbes

Maurice Abisdid-Wagner

Damian Daniels

Walter Wallace, Jr.

Casey Goodson, Jr.

Aiden Ellison

Jonathan Price

Anthony McClain

Rayshard Brooks

Kamal Flowers

James Scurlock

Dion Johnson

Cornelius Fredericks

Breonna Taylor

Ahmaud Arbery

William Green

Atatiana Jefferson

Jaleel wedlock

Ronald Greene

Jassmine McBride

Jewel Roberson

Harith Augustus

Robert White

Dorian Harris

Ronell Foster

Charleena Lyles

Timothy Caughman

Terence Crutcher

Donnell Thompson, Jr.

Alton Sterling

Antronie Scott

Corey Jones

Sandra Bland

Ethel Lance

Depayne Middleton-Doctor

Tywanza Sanders

Norman Cooper

Akai Gurley

Cameron Tillman

Kajieme Powell

Ezell Ford

Eric Garner

Marquise Jones

Deion Fludd

Kimani Gray

Jordan Davis

Darius Simmons

Cletis Williams

Aiyana Stanley-Jones

Julian Alexander

Sean Bell

Alberta Spruill

Amadou Diallo

Mary Mitchell

Edward Gardner

Martin Luther King, Jr.

James Earl Chaney

Andrew Goodman

Michael Schwerner

Herbert Lee

William McDuffie

George Stinney, Jr.* Unfortunately this is not a complete list. (*Say Their Names List 2020 - #SayTheirNames*, 2020)

RESOURCES

Adichie, C. N. (2010). *Half of a yellow sun.* Vintage Canada.

Adichie, C. N. (2015). *We should all be feminists.* Anchor.

Alexander, M. (2020). *The New Jim Crow: Mass Incarceration in the Age of Colorblindness.* The New Press.

Anderson, D. S. (2015). *Emmett till: The murder that shocked the world and propelled the civil rights movement.* Univ. Press of Mississippi.

Andrews-Dwyer, H. (2020, November 16). Ta-Nahesi Coates Not Yet Ready to Celebrate. *The Washington Post*, p. C1.

Angelou, M. (2010). *I know why the caged bird sings*. Random House.

Baldwin, J. (1963). *Go Tell it on the Mountain: The Fire Next Time : If Beale Street Could Talk*.

Berrigan, D. (2009). *The trial of the Catonsville nine*. Fordham University Press.

Blackstock, N. (1975). *Cointelpro: The FBI's Secret War on Political Freedom*. Pathfinder Press.

Bois, W. E. (2007). *The Souls of Black Folk*. OUP Oxford.

Bois, W. E. (2020). *The Souls of Black folk*. Strelbytskyy Multimedia Publishing.

Bolles, R. N., & Brooks, K. (2020). *What color is your parachute? 2021: Your guide to a lifetime of meaningful work and career success*. Ten Speed Press.

Brown, V. (2020, June 29). *Racial justice / Skillful action for a path forward* [Video]. Plum Village.

Cannon, T. (1970). *All Power to the People: The Story of the Black Panther Party*. Peoples Press.

The CIA, contras, gangs, and crack. (2014, May 7).

Carroll, F. (Director). (2020, February). *"Dow Shall Not Kill: The Story of the D.C.Nine"* [TV broadcast]. NPR.

Cleaver, E., & Dell Publishing Company. (1978). *Soul on ice.*

Coates, T. (2015). *Between the world and me.* One World.

Coates, T. (2017). *We were eight years in power: An American tragedy.* One World/Ballantine.

Coates, T. (2019). *The water dancer: A novel.* One World.

Crenshaw, K. (2020). *On Intersectionality: Essential Writings.* The New Press.

Davis, A. Y. (2003). *Are prisons obsolete?* Seven Stories Press.

Davis, A. Y. (2011). *Women, race, & class.* Vintage.

Douglass, F. (2015). *Narrative of the Life of Frederick Douglass.* CreateSpace.

Eddo-Lodge, R. (2020). *Why I'm no longer talking to white people about race.* Bloomsbury Publishing.

Ellison, R. (2018). *Invisible Man*.

Equal Justice Initiative. (2020, June 16). *Lynchings Report*. The Washington Post.

Freire, P. (2014). *Pedagogy of the oppressed: 30th anniversary edition*. Bloomsbury Publishing USA.

Gilmore, R. W. (2007). *Golden Gulag: Prisons, Surplus, Crisis, and Opposition in Globalizing California*. University of California Press.

Giovanni, N. (1996). *Grand mothers: Poems, reminiscences, and short stories about the keepers of our traditions*. Macmillan.

Griffin, J. H. (1976). *Black Like Me*. Signet Book.

Haas, J. (2019). *The assassination of Fred Hampton: How the FBI and the Chicago police murdered a Black Panther*. Chicago Review Press.

Haley, A. (2018). *Roots*. Vintage Classic.

Hampton, F. (1971). *You Can Jail a Revolutionary; But you Can't Jail a Revolution* [Video]. YouTube. https://www.youtube.com/watch?v=YEwv6-SgL0M

The Hangman [Video]. (n.d.). YouTube. www.youtube.com/watdh?v=BRDq7aneXnk</p>

Hanh, T. N. (2001). *Call Me by My True Names: The Collected Poems*. Parallax Press.

Hanh, T. N. (2012). *Please Call Me by My True Names* [Video]. YouTube. https://www.youtube.com/watch?v=JADWkoUpXbQ

Hanh, T. N. (2016). *At Home in the World: Stories and Essential Teachings from a Monk's Life*. Parallax Press.

Hanh, T. N. (2016). *The miracle of mindfulness: An introduction to the practice of meditation*. Beacon Press.

Heartman, C. F. (1915). *Phillis Wheatley (Peters): A critical attempt and a bibliography of her writings*.

(2020, November 16). The Washington Post. https://www.washingtonpost.com/arts-entertainment/2020/11/16/ta-nehisi-coates-between-the-world-and-me/

Hughes, L. (2011). *Selected poems of Langston Hughes*. Vintage.

Hurston, Z. N. (2009). *Mules and Men*. HarperCollins.

Hurston, Z. N. (2020). *Their Eyes Were Watching God*. Prabhat Prakashan.

Iati, M. (2020, September 8). "Taylor Case Led to Rare Spotlight: Police Kill Dozens of Women Yearly." *The Washington Post*, p. A1.

Jacobs, H. A. (1861). *Incidents in the life of a slave girl*. Createspace Independent Publishing Platform.

Jana, T., & Baran, M. (2020). *Subtle acts of exclusion: How to understand, identify, and stop microaggressions*. Berrett-Koehler Publishers.

Johnson, C. (1998). *Middle passage*. Simon & Schuster.

Kendi, I. X. (2016). *Stamped from the beginning: The definitive history of racist ideas in America*. Bold Type Books.

Kendi, I. X. (2019). *How to be an antiracist*. One World/Ballantine.

King, M. L. (1967). *Where do we go from here: Chaos or community?* HarperCollins Publishers.

King, M.L. (1963). *'I have a dream' speech, in its entirety* [Video]. (2010, January 18). NPR.org. https://www.npr.org/2010/01/18/122701268/i-have-a-dream-speech-in-its-entirety.

Lewis, J., & Aydin, A. (2016). *March.*

Lorde, A. (2020). *Sister outsider: Essays and speeches.* Penguin Classics.

Lingo, K. J. (2020, June). *On Racial Equity.*

Lingo, K. J. (2020, December 30). *Spirit rock* | [Video]. Spirit Rock-Honoring the Gifts of 2020 As we Enter the New Year. https://spirit-rock.secure.retreat.guru/?online-program=2467&guest_reg&hash=01bbcb157e0c49bdda4929c-c41c974f4&lang=en

Lorde, A. (2020). *Sister Outsider: Essays and Speeches.* Penguin Classics.

Mandela, N. (2018). *The prison letters of Nelson Mandela.* Liveright Publishing.

Martin Luther King Jr, "Where Do We Go from Here: Chaos or Community?" at the 11th Annual Southern Christian Leadership Conference Convention in Atlanta, 1957) [TV series episode]. (1957).

McCarthy, C. (2014). *I'd rather teach peace*. Orbis Books.

McCarthy, C. (1992). *Solutions to Violence*. Center for Teaching Peace.

McCarthy, C. (2001). *Strength through peace: The ideas and people of nonviolence*. Center for Teaching Peace.

Menakem, R. (2021). *My grandmother's hands: Racialized trauma and the pathway to mending our hearts and bodies*. Penguin UK.

Morrison, T. (1993). *The bluest eye*. Vintage Books.

Morrison, T. (2004). *Beloved: A novel*. Vintage Books.

Obama, B. (2007). *Dreams from my father: A story of race and inheritance*. Broadway Books.

Obama, M. (2018). *Becoming*. Crown Publishing Group (NY).

Obama, M. (2020, August 18). *Speech at Democratic National Convention* [Video]. YouTube. https://www.youtube.com/watch?v=CX9CONduxJs

Owusu, R. Y. (2006). *Kwame Nkrumah's liberation thought: A paradigm for religious advocacy in contemporary Ghana.* Africa World Press.

Ratner, A. A. (Director). (2020). *Kaun* [short film].

Ratner, A.A. (Director). (2019). *All the Difference.*

Rothstein, R. (2017). *The color of law: A forgotten history of how our government segregated America.* Liveright Publishing.

Sanders, H. (1982). *More Than a Renewal:Loretto Before and After VaticanII: 1952-1977.* Sisters of Loretto.

Say Their Names. (2020) https://sayevery.name/say-their-names-list

Seale, B. (1991). *Seize the time: The story of the Black Panther Party and Huey P. Newton.* Black Classic Press.

Shange, N. (2010). *For colored girls who have considered suicide/When the rainbow is enuf.* Simon & Schuster.

Sr Peace/Plum Village. (2020, August 2). *Uncomfortable Spaces:Cultivating Love and Peace for Racial Healing* [Video]. YouTube. https://www.youtube.com/results?search_query=LuDS-B5X9VsY

Stevenson, B. (2014). *Just mercy: A story of justice and redemption.* Spiegel & Grau.

Till-Mobley, M. (2006). *The face of Emmett till.* Dramatic Publishing.

Tropea, J. (Director). (2013). *Hit and Stay* [Film on Anti-war actions].

Walker, A. (2003). *The color purple.* Houghton Mifflin Harcourt.

Walker, A. (2011). *Meridian.* Open Road Media.

Ward, L. (2020). *America's racial karma: An invitation to heal.* Parallax Press.

Ward/The Lotus Institute. (2021, January 15). *Larry Ward's Response to the Insurrection* [Video]. YouTube. https://www.youtube.com/watch?v=dCZlbmA5o1k

Washington, B. T. (1907). *Up From Slavery: an autobiography.* Doubleday, Page & Company.

Wheatley, P. (2001). *Complete writings.* Penguin.

Whitehead, C. (2018). *The Underground Railroad.* Anchor.

Whitehead, C. (2019). *The nickel boys.* Doubleday.

Wilkerson, I. (2020). *Caste: The Origins of our Discontents.* Random House.

Wright, R. (2010). *Black power: Three books from exile: Black power; The color curtain; and white man, listen!* HarperCollins.

Wright, R. (1966). *Native Son.* HarperCollins Publishers.

Wright, R. (2020). *Black Boy [Seventy-fifth Anniversary Edition].* HarperCollins.

X, M. (2015). *The autobiography of Malcolm X.* Ballantine Books.

X, M. (2020). *The end of white world supremacy: Four speeches.* Simon & Schuster.

MY PROFOUND GRATITUDE:

This book would not be necessary without all people whose lives have been twisted and destroyed by racism, discrimination and injustice. Saying their names, keeping their memories, words, acts of resistance and inspiration alive is my goal.

I am grateful for my ancestors, my parents, all the Irish Catholics in my blood family; also my Indigenous, African American, Latinx, Asian and other ancestors whose labor cared for this land and gave us a rich, diverse culture.

I thank all my teachers and mentors - the Sisters of Loretto, all authors, artists, musicians, revolutionaries and all my students, especially my Diversity Workshop leaders, always powerful teachers.

Thich Nhat Hanh and his community continues to teach me mindfulness meditation and ways to speak and act against injustice.

Without the love of my Order of Inter-being and Washington Mindfulness Community brothers and sisters, I would forget that in this present moment, even during the pandemic, I have everything I need for happiness.

African American writers, artists, speakers, leaders, some well-known, many not well enough known, people this book. I hope that I have not mangled or misquoted their message. I encourage readers to go to the original sources, read their words, listen to their speeches, podcasts and music, meet those who are still alive.

To all alcoholics in recovery and those in need of recovery, you inspire me daily to live, to choose a life of equality, generosity, love, service and compassion. Special bows of gratitude to my sponsors and sponsees in recovery.

This book would never have manifested without Seth Godin and Kristin Hatcher's Writing in Community workshop. The Crows, a small group of courageous, generous women writers in WC gave me constant support, encouragement and advice - Kathy, Karena, Cindy, Beverly, Arlette, Margaret, Lisa, Jackie and Laurisa. Also the Equinox Editors Lawrence, Diane, Freddie, Laura, Xiuming, Abbie, Cynthia, Leonardo. You must read all of their books too!

My editor/formatter Michelle Morrow who has guided me through the final process of publishing.

All the healthcare workers, scientists and food providers risking their lives to keep us healthy during this Covid 19 pandemic, thank you. In the words of Alicia Keys, "Good Job!"

Ruth Fishel, my women's retreat partner and author of dozens of books, who has encouraged me to write and publish for many years.

My gratitude for my family is endless. To my parents for my life and love, to my precious brothers and their children and grandchildren, you are the roots, branches and flowers of my life. Thank you Ann and Tom, Bob, Michael, MaryElla, Mike, Vivian, William, Kristen, Amanda, Steven, Eric, Hannah, Avery, Michelle, Dyana, Richard, Ashley, Jordan, John, Tyler and all my cousins, their children and grandchildren.

To my immediate family, I owe my life and daily joy…

Thank you, Vaddey, for being a constant inspiration to transform the suffering of genocide into courage, compassion and wisdom. The beauty of your writing is a gift the world needs. You are the daughter of my heart.

Thank you, Blake, for patience, forgiveness, resilience, encouragement, laughter and love. Your tireless work for equality, freedom and communication to solve conflict, end poverty and the destruction of our planet inspires me. Thank you for choosing me as your mother.

Annelise, you are our hope for a truly multicultural, vibrant, beautiful world. You have been my shining star throughout this writing. Please keep making amazing films, organizing people and saving the world!

And Patrick, my love, my lifeline, my husband, without whom I would often forget to move away from the computer for the last seven months. You feed me, walk me, remind me my body needs to move. You inspire me with your own guitar music, publishing every day, creating new beauty. Thank you for your patience, courage, sustenance, your undying faith, love and support. Life is unimaginable without you.

And to all my friends who are relieved you are not mentioned in this book and to those of you who want to be heard, thank you - and let me know what to write next.

Comments, ideas WELCOME!!!

ABOUT THE AUTHOR

Joann is a peacemaker, meditation teacher, workshop leader, wife, mother, granny, social activist, writer, and mediator.

As a Sister of Loretto for almost twelve years, she taught high school in Alabama and Missouri where she became active in Civil Rights and anti-war activities. She faced thirty-five years in prison for the DC-9 action against Dow Chemical's production of napalm, nerve gas, and defoliants for the war in Vietnam.

50th Anniversary of the Demonstration at Pentagon, 2017

A second teaching career of twenty years in the D.C. and MD public schools enabled her to train hundreds of students to lead diversity workshops, passing her passion for social change to new generations.

She and her husband, a guitarist, teach Qi Gong and meditation and are ordained members of Thich Nhat Hanh's Order of Interbeing. Both love travel, beaches, mountains, walking, reading, writing, retreats, and making "good trouble." She was recently challenged by a beloved family member to climb Old Rag Mountain, just one more time.

Her articles have appeared in *Pathways* and the *Mindfulness Bell* and sections of other books. *Awake from Racism* is her first published book.

Website: www.qicircles.com

Blog: https://joannmalone

Made in the USA
Middletown, DE
05 March 2021